PRAYING
with
PURPOSE

PRAYING *with* PURPOSE

A 28-Day Journey to an Empowered Prayer Life

STEPHEN NELSON RUMMAGE

with Michele Henderson Rummage

Kregel Publications

Praying with Purpose: A 28-Day Journey to an Empowered Prayer Life

© 2006 by Stephen Nelson Rummage

Published by Kregel Publications, a division of Kregel, Inc., P.O. Box 2607, Grand Rapids, MI 49501.

ISBN 0-8254-3651-6

Printed in the United States of America

06 07 08 09 10 / 5 4 3 2 1

To
Joshua Nelson Rummage,
our beloved son,
who prayed daily for us in
family devotion time,
and for whom we have prayed
and will always pray.

CONTENTS

ACKNOWLEDGMENTS

As we wrote this book, Michele and I received great help and encouragement from a number of people.

Dr. Joe Brown, his wife, Teresa, and the wonderful staff and congregation at Hickory Grove Baptist Church have supported us through prayer and kind words. My assistant Monica McKenzie provided valuable help from start to finish. Dr. Chris Griggs, my longtime friend and colleague in ministry, offered keen insights and suggestions along the way. Our parents, Aubrey and Pat Henderson and Gerald and Selma Rummage, have prayed tirelessly on our behalf. To all of these precious people, we are deeply indebted.

I am grateful to God for allowing Michele and me the amazing opportunity to study God's Word together, and to grow in our prayer lives.

—STEPHEN NELSON RUMMAGE

INTRODUCTION

God wants prayer to permeate and saturate your life.

If you lived in the United States after September 11, 2001, you probably noticed the same thing I did: It seemed every Burger King sign was changed from "Whopper Mania" to "Pray for the USA." Driving through the commercial district of a large city the week after the terrorist attacks, I saw signs up and down the boulevard calling for Americans to pray. As the war on terrorism has continued, many business signs still encourage passersby to "Pray for Our Troops." In the aftermath of Hurricane Katrina, our nation rallied to provide for the victims of the storm and flood, and also to lift up the people of New Orleans and the Gulf Coast in prayer.

When has prayer received more overt attention?

A survey conducted by *U.S. News and World Report* indicates that 68 percent of Christians say that they pray more than once a day and an additional 16 percent pray once daily. That means that 84 percent of believers say they pray each day.[1]

What types of things do Christians pray about? The survey shows that:

- 93 percent of Christians pray for God's guidance.
- 91 percent pray to give thanks to God.

- 78 percent pray for health and safety.
- 76 percent pray for God's forgiveness.
- 75 percent pray for general strength.
- 74 percent pray for stronger faith.
- 68 percent pray for their relationships.[2]

Most believers take prayer seriously. They call on God, expecting that He will answer. Yet, the majority of Christians desire something more from their prayer lives than what they now experience. Many believers have told me that the spiritual discipline they most want to strengthen is prayer. Parents want to learn how to pray for their teenagers. Newlyweds are working to build their marriages around prayer. Pastors desire prayer-empowered ministries, and all sorts of people just want to pray more effectively.

So you are like most Christians if you are dissatisfied with your prayers and want prayer to play a larger part in your life. We understand that God works through prayer. We pray believing that God hears and answers when we cry out to Him. For the growing believer in Jesus Christ, prayer isn't only something to do at the table before eating a meal or when rising in the morning and before going to sleep at night or even in times of solitude and meditation. We share God's desire that prayer become central in our lives. We know that God longs for our lives to be filled with prayer. We experience His purpose as we pray. We understand that God wants prayer to be central to everything we do and all that we are.

In 1 Thessalonians 5:17, the apostle Paul instructs believers: "Pray without ceasing" as translated in the New King James Version. Other contemporary translations use other words to convey the thought, such as "pray continually" (NIV), "keep on praying" (NLT), and "pray all the time" (MSG). No matter how you say it, God tells us to keep on praying . . . without ceasing . . . continually . . . all the time. What a strong command!

How do we obey this aspect of God's Word? Should we keep our heads bowed and our eyes closed when we're walking down the sidewalk or driving our cars? If not, what does God mean? I see two major implications in this command.

First, God wants us to pray at every opportunity. Time in prayer cannot be a hit-and-miss, sporadic event if we want to make spiritual progress. Instead, our prayer must be regular and continual. Prayer has to be a disciplined habit. George Müller revitalized the nineteenth-century English church simply by founding orphanages, totally on faith and prayer, for thousands of children. Asked how much time he spent in prayer, he replied, "Hours every day. But I live in the spirit of prayer. I pray as I walk and when I lie down and when I arise."

God wants us to see every opportunity as an occasion to pray.

Second, God wants us to live and breathe in an atmosphere of prayer. As you make prayer a consistent practice, you will discover that your heart and mind will begin to gravitate almost instinctively to prayer.

A fish swimming in the water is in its ideal atmosphere. The fish doesn't wake up in the morning and think, "I believe I'll go swimming today." Because water is the fish's environment, its only possible response is to swim. In the same way, God wants prayer to become our environment, as natural to us as breathing. The more we pray, the more we will want to pray. As we go about our daily business, we'll find ourselves calling on God's name. When we stir from sleep in the morning, we'll awake talking to the Lord. Prayer will be an indispensable part of our personalities.

God wants you to learn how to pray with purpose. The intention of this book is to help you fulfill your desire to become a Christian of unceasing and focused prayer. The book is divided into five parts. The first four parts take you on a journey into a more empowered prayer life. The last part answers some questions you may ask along the journey.

I suggest that the way to get the most benefit from this book is to read the first four parts over a period of twenty-eight days. Each part examines a different aspect of prayer. Part 1 presents principles from the prayer life of Jesus. Part 2 teaches us from the prayers of an Old Testament woman named Hannah. In part 3, we'll notice the specifics of how David sought God's forgiveness and cleansing through prayer. Part 4 is a phrase-by-phrase study of the Lord's Prayer.

The studies in part 2 on Hannah's prayer were written by my lifelong prayer partner, my wife, Michele. She brings a woman's perspective to the powerful story of a woman's triumphant prayers. The personal references in chapters 8 through 14 are in Michele's voice. The rest of the personal references in the book are in my voice.

The daily readings will take you no longer than half an hour to read each day. Each reading also includes a suggested Scripture reading and a prayer guide.

The final section addresses ten questions about prayer. If you have asked, "Why should I pray?" or "Why hasn't God answered my prayer?" here are some answers. The last question—"How can I pray to become a Christian?"—is essential to having any meaningful communication with God. If you have not trusted Christ as your Savior, my prayer is that this book might lead you to long for a relationship with Him; you can turn to that last part right now and consider God's wonderful plan for you in Jesus Christ.

May God bless you richly as you begin your journey in prayer.

Part 1

JESUS'S PRAYER LIFE

Principles for Praying with Purpose
God works through prayer.
Busy people can pray.
God desires your requests.
Jesus's name opens doors.
Authentic prayer produces surrender.

Day 1

A Life Filled with Prayer

What if you woke tomorrow morning to discover that you had all the power of God?

The winds and waves obeyed your command. You could make deaf people hear and blind people see. You could even raise the dead.

Would you still feel the need to pray?

Jesus did.

I once took an old hardcover Bible and marked every reference to Jesus praying. It was amazing to see how often the Gospel writers spoke of the Lord praying. Sometimes He went off alone to a solitary spot on a mountainside. On other occasions, He prayed aloud among His followers. He prayed as He prepared to make important decisions, such as calling the Twelve. He instructed them to pray so that they might have God's power in their lives.

Within His body, Jesus had all of the power and authority of God, yet He prayed. His prayer life sets a perfect example of how a person should live in communion with God. But His prayers were not offered just for the sake of providing an example. His prayers were real. He lived by prayer.

E. M. Bounds, who spent his lifetime studying and writing about prayer, wrote, "Prayer filled the life of our Lord while on earth.

His life was a constant stream of incense sweet and perfumed by prayer."[1]

This week, we examine some significant events in the prayer life of Jesus. We will not cover all aspects of His prayer life; to master the Lord's prayer life could take years of intense study. Instead, we'll look at a few examples of Jesus's practice of prayer and His teaching about prayer.

SUGGESTED SCRIPTURE READING

Philippians 2:5–11

PRAYER GUIDE

The Bible commands us, "Let this mind [attitude] be in you which was also in Christ Jesus" (Phil. 2:5). As you pray,

- ask God to help you develop the kind of attitude Jesus had.
- commit to obeying whatever God commands in His Word.
- thank God for the honor of coming before Him in prayer.
- praise God for giving His Son, Jesus Christ.

Day 2

WHILE HE PRAYED

> When all the people were baptized,
> it came to pass that Jesus also was
> baptized; and while He prayed, the
> heaven was opened. (Luke 3:21)

> If we pray little, it is probably be-
> cause we do not really believe that
> prayer accomplishes much at all.
> —Wayne Grudem[1]

God works through prayer.

Oscar and Helen lived out in the country near Slippery Rock, Pennsylvania, about fifty miles north of Pittsburgh. A man in his late sixties, Oscar was driving his tractor too close to the edge of a ravine. The tractor slid, the grade became too steep, and the tractor flipped, landing on top of him.

From the house, Helen saw it happen, but what could she do? The tractor was far too heavy for her to lift off her husband. The nearest neighbor was miles down the road. She phoned her sons, who lived some distance away. They promised to come quickly, but they'd never make it in time. Helen rushed down to Oscar's side, petrified that he would be crushed under the weight of the tractor.

As she walked, Helen kept praying, "Lord, please send someone to help."

Suddenly, a man Helen had never seen before came up behind her and asked, "How can I help?"

Helen quickly told the man what had happened. The man went into the ravine and simply heaved the tractor off Oscar. The sons arrived. They scrambled to make sure Oscar was all right. Helen turned around to thank the man, but he was gone. She looked down the road. No car was in sight. To the end of her life, Helen believed that God had sent an angel to rescue her husband.[2]

Whether the stranger who appeared was an angel, it is certain that God worked mightily to answer Helen's prayer.

CONVERSATION WITH GOD

How does prayer work? For growing Christians, prayer is more than self-talk or personal meditation. Prayer is conversation with the living God. Conversation is always two-way communication. We pray believing that God hears and answers. In response to our prayers, God increases our trust in Him. He does His intended work in coordination with the prayers of His people.

Theologian Wayne Grudem makes an audacious statement that has biblical warrant: "Prayer changes the way God acts."[3] Perhaps you've never thought about it that way, but it's true. God—who is all-powerful and all-knowing, who has ordained and established the universe, who governs time and eternity—has chosen to work through your prayers.

When we truly come to believe that God changes the world and works in our lives through prayer, we will pray with purpose. In Luke 3, we encounter Luke's first recorded instance of Jesus praying. We don't know the words that He said, but we do see how God worked in response to His prayer.

A MAN NAMED JOHN

I invite you to travel almost two thousand years into the past, to the region of Judea in the land of Israel. Out by the meandering Jordan, large groups of people are crowding the riverbanks to listen to a preacher. They call him *The Baptizer.* The Baptizer's given name is John—a common name in those days. Everything about John, however, seems extraordinary:

> The word of God came to John the son of Zacharias in the wilderness. And he went into all the region around the Jordan, preaching a baptism of repentance for the remission of sins, as it is written in the book of the words of Isaiah the prophet, saying: "The voice of one crying in the wilderness: 'Prepare the way of the LORD; Make His paths straight.'" (Luke 3:2b–4)

We would call John's appearance unusual. He lives out in the backwoods, so he looks wooly. His unruly beard is marked with the sticky remnants of locusts and wild honey, the cuisine he eats each day. He wears coarse clothing made from camel's hair, with his clothing cinched around his waist with a leather strap. John does not look like the kind of guy you'd sit beside in church. He's a wild man.

John's preaching is even more striking than his strange appearance. His basic message? *Repent.* He is commanding his audience to change their lives radically. And he's not afraid to be specific about the kind of changes they need to make. He tells people who have extra clothes and food to give to the needy. He tells soldiers not to intimidate people. He instructs tax collectors to stop overcharging.

When the Jewish religious leaders come out to scrutinize his message, he calls them snakes. He rebukes King Herod for marrying his brother's wife. Nothing frightens John into silence. The people love such honest preaching, and masses come to hear him. With passion, he calls people to get their hearts ready for the coming of God's kingdom. Then, he plunges them into the waters of the Jordan River as a sign of their repentance.

ENTER, JESUS

The Pharisees and other religious leaders keep asking John, "Who are you?" Some speculate that he might claim to be the Messiah. No, he tells them, "I am 'The voice of one crying in the wilderness: "Make straight the way of the LORD,"' as the prophet Isaiah said" (John 1:23). John's goal is to get people ready for the coming of the Messiah. He tells those who follow him, "I'm baptizing you with water, but Someone is coming after me who will baptize you with the Holy Spirit. He's mightier than I am. In fact, I'm not even worthy to carry His sandals" (vv. 26–27, author's paraphrase).

Soon after he says that, John sees Jesus walking toward him, asking to be baptized. John recognizes Jesus as the One God had promised and wonders at the request for someone sinless to be baptized. Luke's description of Jesus's baptism says:

> When all the people were baptized, it came to pass that Jesus also was baptized; and while He prayed, the heaven was opened. And the Holy Spirit descended in bodily form like a dove upon Him, and a voice came from heaven which said, "You are My beloved Son; in You I am well pleased." Now Jesus Himself began His ministry at about thirty years of age. (Luke 3:21–23a)

What a scene that must have been—the inauguration of Jesus's earthly ministry. Though He had been God's Son from eternity and though He had been sent as Israel's Redeemer and Messiah, Jesus's work began in earnest at that moment.

PRAYER: THE STARTING PLACE

Jesus began His earthly ministry praying. As He called out to His Father, the heavens were opened. We've all experienced the delight of watching the clouds part on a gloomy day to let through the sunshine. What happened at Jesus's baptism, however, was much greater than an atmospheric event. It was a spiritual phenomenon. God opened heaven at that moment to reveal Himself and to bear witness to His Son.

By initiating His ministry with prayer, Jesus provides the perfect example for all believers. Prayer is the starting place of your spiritual life. God begins and continues His work in you through prayer. Believers have been given "every spiritual blessing in the heavenly places in Christ" (Eph. 1:3b). The riches of heaven are yours. Think for a few moments about how God opens heaven for Christians through prayer.

First, God Works Through Prayer to Bring Believers into His Family

At Jesus's baptism, God the Father Himself testified to Jesus as His beloved Son. In turn, Jesus graciously calls believers His brothers and sisters in God's eternal family. "Whoever does the will of My Father in heaven," Jesus says, "is My brother and sister and mother" (Matt. 12:50).

God says, "You are all sons of God through faith in Christ Jesus" (Gal. 3:26). When you prayed and asked Jesus for the gift of salvation, your words were probably not eloquent. You may have stammered, searching for the right things to say. That prayer, however, was certainly the most important and powerful prayer you will ever pray. The moment you prayed, "Lord, save me," God changed you forever!

Becoming a Christian is not merely a human decision to affiliate with the church or even to accept a set of truths about God. Instead, salvation revolutionizes our eternal destination and our very identity. The Bible says, "Whoever calls on the name of the LORD shall be saved" (Rom. 10:13).

When you called on the Lord, admitting your sinfulness to Him and trusting in Jesus alone to give you forgiveness of sin and eternal life, God saved you and brought you into His family. Before, you were a spiritual orphan, outside the household of God. Now, you are God's adopted child.

Fatherlessness in America has been called an epidemic. More than one-third of children in the United States live apart from their fathers.[4] Increasingly, people are coming to faith in Christ who have distant or even hostile relationships with their earthly fathers. Now more than ever, believers need to understand and embrace the beautiful reality of our position as children of God. You have a personal and loving relationship with your Father in heaven. You can call on Him in prayer, knowing that He will hear and answer the voice of His child.

As God's child, keep these things in mind when you pray:

- You have perfect security because you are eternally adopted into God's family.
- God is supremely concerned about the daily concerns of your life.
- There's nothing you can't talk to God about.

In reply to our prayer asking Him for salvation, God has brought us into His family. Notice a second way that God opens heaven through prayer:

God Also Has Sent His Holy Spirit to Live Inside You

As Jesus was being baptized, the Holy Spirit descended on Him in the form of a dove. Many Bible scholars have noted that the picture of Jesus, God's Son, coming up from the waters of the Jordan as God the Father speaks and as God the Holy Spirit comes down is a powerful and unmistakable picture of the Trinity.

The same Holy Spirit that descended upon Jesus at His baptism came to live in you the moment you were saved. God says: "You are not in the flesh but in the Spirit, if indeed the Spirit of God dwells in you. Now if anyone does not have the Spirit of Christ, he is not His" (Rom. 8:9). To have a saving relationship with Jesus Christ is to have the Holy Spirit.

The Bible calls your body "the temple of the Holy Spirit who is in you, whom you have from God" (1 Cor. 6:19b). The indwelling

Holy Spirit is a mystery, a wonder, and a miracle. The mystery is that the Spirit of Holy God could come to live in sinful men and women. The wonder is that the Spirit of Almighty God can reside within our puny bodies. The miracle is that the Spirit of Infinite God would make His home within us. The reality of the Holy Spirit living within us is beyond amazing, but it's exactly what happened when God saved us.

The indwelling Holy Spirit will assist you in praying the right way and for the right things. God says, "The Spirit also helps in our weaknesses. For we do not know what we should pray for as we ought, but the Spirit Himself makes intercession for us with groanings which cannot be uttered" (Rom. 8:26).

Sometimes we don't know how to pray in a situation because our perspective is imperfect. Our spiritual immaturity and limited minds keep us from praying in consistency with God's will. Other times, we simply don't know the words to say when we pray. It is during those times that the Holy Spirit speaks to God for us. He calls out to God on our behalf and expresses deep feelings that words cannot explain.

As you pray, consider a few implications concerning the indwelling Holy Spirit:

- You can trust in the Holy Spirit to direct your prayers toward God's will.
- You can depend on the Holy Spirit to convict you of sins as you pray.
- You can trust the Holy Spirit to show you what you most need to pray for.

We need to consider one more way God works through prayer:

God Initiates Our Service to Him Through Prayer

Luke tells us that, following His baptism, Jesus "began His ministry" (Luke 3:23). You also have entered into the everlasting service of the Lord as a believer in Christ. God has a special purpose and plan for your life that He will unfold as you prayerfully follow Him.

God says, "Let us run with endurance the race that is set before us" (Heb. 12:1). God has placed a race in front of you. That race is your service to Him and His purpose for you. It's a unique race. No believer's purpose is exactly like anyone else's. It's something God designed with you in mind.

In His ministry, Jesus fulfilled God's purpose as He worked amazing miracles, poured His life into others, met the needs of hurting people, and finally died on the cross. God's purpose for your life includes trials as well as triumphs, days of heartbreak and times of rejoicing. In everything He has planned, God wants to use you to His glory. You fulfill His plan for your life as you seek God in prayer. Our ministry before God involves surrendering ourselves to Him and receiving guidance from Him as we pray.

Remember the following truths about your service to God while you pray:

- God has a definite purpose for you.
- God's purpose for you will require facing personal sacrifices in the spiritual power only God can give.
- God's purpose for you is the best life you could ever experience.

THE WALK SIGNAL

It's a classic *Peanuts* cartoon. Snoopy the beagle steps up to a crosswalk and reads a message posted there: "To cross street push button . . . wait for *walk* signal."

Snoopy pushes the button, turns toward the street, and waits. And waits. And waits.

Finally, Linus walks past Snoopy and says, "You have to move your feet, too."

As he walks across the street, Snoopy grins and says, "How embarrassing!"[5]

God has given you the *walk* signal in your prayer life. The pathway of prayer is open. Now is not the time to stand around; it's time to begin experiencing God's amazing power and plan. He has made the way for you to live by prayer. He has given you access to Himself through prayer. Now, He's waiting on you to claim your birthright as a child of God.

He's waiting on you to pray.

SUGGESTED SCRIPTURE READING

Romans 8

PRAYER GUIDE

If Christ is your Savior, thank God for heavenly riches:

- He has made you righteous in Christ.
- He has sent His Spirit to live in you.
- He has adopted you as His child.
- He has made the way for you to pray.
- He has promised that nothing will separate you from His love.

Day 3

HE OFTEN WITHDREW AND PRAYED

So He Himself [Jesus] often withdrew into the wilderness and prayed. (Luke 5:16)

I am so busy now that if I did not spend two or three hours each day in prayer, I would not get through the day.

—Martin Luther[1]

*B*usy people *can* pray.

We have to be reminded of that occasionally. If we are not careful, busyness can conquer our prayer lives.

When I take a retreat or an extended vacation, I often find myself praying more deeply and meaningfully. In the leisure of being away from household responsibilities, church duties, and the workaday routine, I savor time alone with God. I commit myself to continue praying in the same way once I return to "normal life."

Then I return home, get back to work, and "normal life" happens.

I become busy with all the stuff I have to do. Most of us have lives filled with more stuff than a turkey on the Thanksgiving table. It may be good stuff. It may be stuff that needs to be done. A lot of it may be stuff in service to God. But, because of all that stuff, we find ourselves drawn away from the quiet place of prayer.

TOO BUSY?

A big part of the problem may be that we can simply become *too* busy. A friend loves to remind me that busyness is not necessarily a virtue.

A hectic schedule can become a way of avoiding God and the meaning of our lives. D. L. Moody said, "If you have so much business to attend to that you have no time to pray, depend upon it, you have more business on hand than God ever intended you should have."[2]

Busyness will not only hurt you spiritually; it can also keep you from helping others effectively. One Christian couple began to develop a close relationship with their neighbors, hoping to lead them to Christ. When these believers had opportunity to talk to their friends about the Lord, they were surprised by the neighbors' response: "We couldn't be Christians; we couldn't live at your pace." The couple was attracted to Jesus but scared by the busyness they saw in their Christian friends' lives.[3]

Christians would benefit from examining the flurry of our activities and asking, "Does God really want me to be doing all of this?" Much of our busyness, however, does seem unavoidable. Most of us would be pressed to identify the surplus things we could erase to be less busy.

So, how can busy people fit prayer into their lives?

Can a mother with three children—who is alone only if she locks herself in the bathroom—take time for any prayer longer than, "*Lord, help me*"?

Does a college student who has a full load of classes, an internship, and a part-time job ever find time for meaningful prayer?

Is a person who works ten to twelve hours a day able to reserve sufficient energy to seek God in prayer?

Yet busy people can pray. Jesus proved that. Though His life was demanding, Jesus lingered long in prayer.

Luke described Jesus's practice of prayer, that "He Himself often withdrew into the wilderness and prayed" (Luke 5:16). The language Luke uses in both the verbs *withdrew* and *prayed* indicates that Jesus was engaged habitually in the practice of slipping away from the crowds that surrounded Him and pouring out His soul to God in prayer. In his wonderful book, *The Life of Christ,* James Stalker observed that "In His busiest period, when He was often so tired with the labors of the day that at the approach of evening He was ready to fling Himself down in utter fatigue, He would nevertheless escape away from the crowds and His disciples to the mountain-top, and spend the whole night in lonely communion with His Father."[4]

Sometimes in the early morning hours and sometimes throughout the night, He spent significant time in prayer regularly. Jesus's example teaches busy believers to pray consistently and meaningfully.

PRAYING ON A BUSY SCHEDULE

Jesus didn't let grass grow under His sandals. He was a busy man.

When I read the accounts of Jesus's life in the Gospels, I am often surprised by how action packed and fast paced His days were. He was constantly on the go and in demand, persistently interrupted by people with needs and relentlessly tested by opponents.

Jesus had a lot to do, yet He took time to pray.

The first chapter of Mark's gospel describes what might have been a typical Sabbath day for Jesus while He stayed in the Galilean town of Capernaum. He went to the synagogue where He preached (Mark 1:21–22) and cast out an unclean spirit from a demon-possessed man (vv. 23–26). Later Jesus traveled to the home of Simon Peter and Andrew, two of His earliest disciples. Upon discovering that Peter's mother-in-law was sick with a fever, Jesus healed her (vv. 29–31). By evening, people from the entire city gathered at the door, looking on as Jesus healed the sick and cast out demons (vv. 32–34). Throughout the day, people had been pulling Jesus in every direction, vying for His attention.

If the Sabbath was so eventful, imagine how busy His other days must have been. He went to bed tired that night, knowing that the next day was likely to be even more rigorous.

After such a hard day, it would have been understandable if Jesus had decided to sleep late the next morning. Instead, He woke up early to pray: "Now in the morning, having risen a long while before daylight, He went out and departed to a solitary place; and there He prayed" (v. 35). Though He was physically drained from the previous day's ministry and though another grueling day awaited, Jesus roused Himself from sleep in the early morning hours. He walked out to a quiet place where He could be alone. There, He met with His Father in prayer.

PRAYER PRINCIPLES FOR BUSY PEOPLE

This episode in the life of Jesus illustrates two principles that can make a tremendous difference in our lives: First, busy people must make time for prayer, and second, busy people must put a hedge around their prayer lives, so they aren't distracted.

Busy People Must Make Time for Prayer

Your prayer life won't just happen. A more intimate communion with God won't come by accident. If you want to grow into a person of prayer, you have to make the effort and take the time.

Jesus was not haphazard in His approach to prayer. He deliberately and sacrificially set aside time to spend with the Father. Notice the load-bearing phrases in Mark 1:35: "Now in the morning . . . a long while before daylight . . . He prayed."

Jesus chose to pray before the rush of His day began. In doing so, He exemplified the words of the psalmist: "My voice You shall hear in the morning, O LORD; in the morning I will direct it to You, and I will look up" (Ps. 5:3). Many Christians have followed this same pattern, waking in the early hours to spend time with God.

Someone might argue that prayer does not have to be confined to the early morning hours. However, it is true that devoting the first waking minutes of the day to prayer helps to strengthen one's prayer life. While prayer does us good at whatever hour we pray, many believers have discovered that the consistent practice of early morning prayer can make all the difference in their day.

Jesus shows us that busy people must take time for prayer. Before you read any further, consider a few questions:

- Are you deliberately making time for prayer, or are you giving God the leftover time after all of your other daily business is done?
- Do you give God the best part of your day—when you have energy and a fresh mind with which to concentrate—or are you praying when you are worn out?
- With all of the demands of your schedule in mind, how can you intentionally make time for prayer in your day?

Busy People Also Must Guard Against Distractions from Prayer

When you determine to pray, you can count on something or someone trying to interrupt your time with God. Jesus faced disruptions from his prayer time in the person of Simon Peter. "And Simon and those who were with Him searched for Him. When they found Him, they said to Him, 'Everyone is looking for You'" (Mark 1:36–37).

Peter woke up that morning, discovered that Jesus wasn't in the house, and panicked. More sick people waited to be healed, more demon-possessed people needed to be delivered, and eager listeners would be gathering to hear Jesus teach.

"Where in the world is Jesus?" Peter wondered.

After tracking Jesus down, Peter gently scolded Jesus for being out of reach when everyone was looking for Him. Can you imagine being so rude as to barge in on God's Son during His prayer time, and then to set His day's agenda? Peter had not yet learned that Jesus did not allow the wishes of others to determine His plan. Jesus's reply shows that God alone controlled His appointment book: "Let us go into the next towns, that I may preach there also, because for this purpose I have come forth" (Mark 1:38). Jesus was saying, "Peter, only My Father in heaven determines My priorities. No one else is competent enough to order My day. I have begun My day by talking to the Father. I'll continue My day by obeying the Father. The Father has directed Me onward to the next towns."

Consider the enormous pressures that could have pulled Jesus away from hearing and obeying the heavenly Father in prayer:

- People He loved, like Peter, were interrupting.
- Real, pressing needs tugged at Him.
- Even His own desire to be busy doing God's work could have distracted Him.

Instead of listening to the myriad voices that called Him away from prayer, however, Jesus chose to heed the Voice that beckoned Him to the quiet place of fellowship with God.

Martin Luther's barber and longtime friend once asked him how a Christian should pray. Luther responded with a long letter detailing his own prayer practice. One of the things Luther advised was to avoid distractions: "Guard yourself carefully against those false, deluding ideas which tell you, 'Wait a little while. I will pray in an hour; first I must attend to this or that.' Such thoughts get you away from prayer into other affairs which so hold your attention and involve you that nothing comes of prayer for that day."[5]

Distractions can come from without, but they more often come from within. Stray thoughts flutter around in the mind like butterflies in a meadow. And, like a puppy dog chasing those butterflies, we allow our concentration to stray off to pursue the distractions.

Fellowship with God can be interrupted by, "I wonder what we'll be having for dinner tonight," or "I need to have the oil changed in my car today," or "I hope I can finish the project I'm working on at the office."

From time to time, every believer needs to examine his or her life to ask:

- What usually keeps me from praying the way I need to pray?
- What are the most common distractions I face in my prayer time?
- Why do I pay attention to these distractions?
- What can I do in the future to keep my prayer time focused?

PLAYING SCALES

In the world of classical music, Irish flutist James Galway is a superstar. When he was nearly fifty years of age, Galway began to feel that his technique on the instrument was slipping a bit. He was determined not to fall into the trap of "getting old and famous and playing bad concerts," so he decided to start practicing scales. He played up and down the scales of each key, like any beginning flutist could do.

At his first practice session, playing scale after scale, Galway was shocked to discover how out of shape he was. "I could play concertos and repertory pieces with ease," he said, "but the scales were stiff, and they were inconsistent from key to key." Thereafter, day after day until his proficiency improved, James Galway, the world renowned master of the flute, played scales.

Jesus Christ never left the basics in His relationship with His Father in heaven. Time alone with God was essential to His life. Though He was extremely busy, He made time to pray and let nothing distract Him from it.

He's calling you to that same basic commitment. He wants your vow: "Lord, I won't let busyness keep me from prayerfulness."

SUGGESTED SCRIPTURE READING

Psalm 5

PRAYER GUIDE

When you bring requests before the Father,

- ask Him to show you parts of your schedule you should lay aside for His sake.
- ask for direction to a time you can consistently spend in meaningful prayer daily.
- ask for strength to keep your "prayer appointment" with Him.
- ask for protection from distractions in prayer.

Day 4

ASK ... SEEK ... KNOCK

I say to you, ask, and it will be given
to you; seek, and you will find;
knock, and it will be opened to you.
(Luke 11:9)

Pray the largest prayers. You cannot
think a prayer so large that God, in
answering it, will not wish you had
made it larger. Pray not for crutches,
but for wings!

—Phillips Brooks[1]

God desires your requests.

When you pray, He wants you to ask Him to meet specific needs
in your life. Asking is not selfish or presumptuous. When believers
fail to ask God in prayer, we miss His best for our lives.

Someone has imaginatively described millions of rooms in heaven
filled with large boxes. Each box is beautifully wrapped, decorated
with brightly colored ribbons, and labeled with a name. Inside the
boxes are answers never delivered to believers on earth because they
were never requested in prayer.

A vital spiritual truth is conveyed in this story. God's Word teaches that a large part of prayer is asking and receiving. When we fail to ask in prayer, we fail to receive.

BOLDNESS TO ASK

Believers who grow strong in prayer discover that God wants His children to make courageous requests of Him. God says, "You do not have because you do not ask" (James 4:2d). We can "ask amiss" when our requests are prompted by ungodly desires (v. 3). God knows when our motives are self-centered. All the same, God intends for us to bring our deepest needs to Him in prayer.

God wants us to ask for His direction. When young Solomon became king of Israel, God extended to him an invitation to ask anything: "The LORD appeared to Solomon in a dream by night; and God said, 'Ask! What shall I give you?' (1 Kings 3:5). Solomon received great wisdom—along with other blessings he did not request—because he simply responded to God's desire that he ask. The same spiritual insight Solomon received is available to all believers. God's Word assures us that we can ask God for wisdom, expecting to receive it: "If any of you lacks wisdom, let him ask of God, who gives to all liberally and without reproach, and it will be given to him" (James 1:5).

God also wants us to ask Him for the daily needs of our lives. He spoke to the drought-stricken nation of Israel and commanded the people to ask for His provision for a pressing physical concern: "Ask the LORD for rain in the time of the latter rain. The LORD will make flashing clouds; He will give them showers of rain, grass in the field for everyone" (Zech. 10:1). The people received the rain when they asked because their request was in line with God's will. When we ask for our needs, we are not guaranteed that God will always answer in the way we expect. Our prayers may not initially correspond to His purposes. He often uses our asking to align our lives and desires to His best plans for us. John writes: "Now this is the confidence that we have in Him, that if we ask anything according to His will, He hears us" (1 John 5:14).

God also desires to ease our anxiety and grant us peace. Paul writes, "Be anxious for nothing, but in everything by prayer and supplication, with thanksgiving, let your requests be made known to God" (Phil. 4:6). The terms he uses, such as *prayer, supplication,* and *requests,* are all petition words. What happens when we make supplication and requests to God? He gives us tranquility in our hearts: "And the peace of God, which surpasses all understanding, will guard your hearts and minds through Christ Jesus" (v. 7).

The reality of asking and receiving from God in prayer is an overarching biblical truth. It's no surprise that the Lord Jesus would instruct us to make requests of God. When His disciples asked Him to teach them to pray, one of the things Jesus stressed was the importance of asking. His words are simple but powerful: "Ask . . . seek . . . knock" (Luke 11:9). We will examine each command, but first, let's consider two parables Jesus told about asking in prayer. In Luke 11, the Lord framed the commands *ask, seek,* and *knock* with two vivid analogies that draw pictures of how God responds to His children's requests.

GREATER THAN A FRIEND

The story Jesus tells in Luke 11 is sometimes known as "The Parable of the Persistent Neighbor." It's about a man who needs to borrow bread from his neighbor at a very inconvenient hour. Has a neighbor ever come to your house to borrow a scoop of coffee or a cup of sugar? That doesn't happen as often as it once did. Even if we did need food from a neighbor, we wouldn't be so rude as to ring the doorbell at midnight. Jesus's parable refers to things outside our normal life experiences:

> Which of you shall have a friend, and go to him at midnight and say to him, "Friend, lend me three loaves; for a friend of mine has come to me on his journey, and I have nothing to set before him"; and he will answer from within and say, "Do not trouble me; the door is now shut, and my children

are with me in bed; I cannot rise and give to you"? I say to you, though he will not rise and give to him because he is his friend, yet because of his persistence he will rise and give him as many as he needs. (Luke 11:5–8)

Three main characters appear in this parable, a weary traveler, a persistent friend, and a grumpy neighbor. Let's think about each one for a few moments.

First, consider the *weary traveler.* He probably began his journey in the cool of the afternoon and continued through the evening. Most travelers in those times avoided being on the road during the hottest hours of daylight. Now that he has arrived, his legs and back are tired; his feet are sore. He hasn't eaten since he left home. Near midnight, he threads his way to an old friend's house, knowing that his friend will give him some food for his stomach and a bed to sleep on.

We now meet the traveler's *persistent friend.* He hears a familiar voice outside his house, opens the door, and discovers his buddy from out of town. But panic grips him as he invites the visitor into his house. Tradition, culture, and hospitality all dictate that he must invite his friend to stay for the night—which is no problem—and that he give him something to eat before bed—which is a big problem. His family has already eaten all their bread for that day, and no more will be baked until morning. In desperation, he slips away from his hungry guest, goes to a nearby house, and pounds on the door.

This brings us to the *grumpy neighbor.* He and his family are all asleep in their little house. Like most of the other homes in the village, his house has only one room. Two-thirds of that little room is on ground level; the other third is raised slightly. On the raised part, a charcoal stove burns to keep the family warm. The man, his wife, and children are all gathered around that stove, sleeping on mats. Suddenly, he wakes to hear someone knocking on the door.

He calls out in an irritable stage whisper, "Who is it?"

His friend says, "It's me! I have a guest who just arrived. I need three loaves."

The man inside calls back, "Are you kidding? Go away. We're sleeping in here!"

The man keeps knocking.

The grumpy neighbor calls out, "Will you cut that out? You're going to wake everybody in the house."

But the persistent friend keeps on knocking.

Finally, the grumpy neighbor gets up. He tiptoes around his sleeping wife and children. He shuffles across the cottage floor, grabs three loaves from a basket, fumbles with the latch, shoves his hand through the partly opened door, and says, "Here! Take the bread and go home!"

You can almost see Jesus's eyes sparkling as He finishes the story: "Though he will not rise and give to him because he is his friend, yet because of his persistence he will rise and give him as many as he needs" (Luke 11:8). The Greek word translated "persistence" can mean "shamelessness or audacity." The persistent friend received the bread from his grumpy neighbor because he was not ashamed to make a nuisance of himself. He had the audacity to make a bold request.

The point of this story is *not* that God has to be pestered into answering. Instead, Jesus is saying that if a grumpy guy will grant a request from a persistent friend, then surely our loving heavenly Father will supply our needs when we ask. He's greater than a friend, and He wants us to ask, seek, and knock.

MORE CARING THAN A FATHER

In another, more brief parable, found in Luke 11:11–13, Jesus compares a believer making requests of God in prayer with a child asking something of a father:

> If a son asks for bread from any father among you, will he give him a stone? Or if he asks for a fish, will he give him a serpent instead of a fish? Or if he asks for an egg, will he offer him a scorpion? If you then, being evil, know how to

give good gifts to your children, how much more will your heavenly Father give the Holy Spirit to those who ask Him!

Again, Jesus is illustrating how God responds to our petitions. Imagine that a hungry little boy asks his dad for a slice of bread. What would the dad's natural response be? He might give him the bread, or he might say, "Not right now, son. You'll ruin your dinner." But he wouldn't hand the child a round, brown stone that looks like a yeast roll and say, "Here, kid, sink your teeth into this!" That would be cruel. Or, what if a youngster asks his father for a fish stick or a pickled, hard-boiled egg? Dad might say, "Wouldn't you rather have a peanut-butter sandwich?" Only a vicious father, though, would hand his son a slithering snake or a stinging scorpion to eat instead.

The point is, when a child requests something, a parent may say "yes," "no," or, "I've got something better for you." But no caring parent would meet a child's request with an answer that is deliberately harmful. Jesus concludes the analogy by saying: "If you then, being evil, know how to give good gifts to your children, how much more will your heavenly Father give the Holy Spirit to those who ask Him!" (Luke 11:13). In Matthew's account of this story, Jesus broadens the gifts of God beyond the Holy Spirit, saying, "How much more will your Father who is in heaven give good things to those who ask Him!" (Matt. 7:11b).

Billy Graham has said, "Prayer to God is like a child's conversation with his father. It is natural for a child to ask his father for the things he needs."[2] All human moms and dads are sinful by nature. Even so, most parents try to give good gifts to their children. Unlike human parents, God is perfect in His goodness, wisdom, and power. He is more caring than any father on earth. He will not fail to give the Holy Spirit and all other good gifts to His children when we ask, seek, and knock. We can have complete confidence in Him.

THREE SIMPLE COMMANDS

Tucked in the middle of these two parables are Jesus's commandments for bold and persistent prayer: "So I say to you, ask, and it will be given to you; seek, and you will find; knock, and it will be opened to you. For everyone who asks receives, and he who seeks finds, and to him who knocks it will be opened" (Luke 11:9–10).

Perhaps you have been introduced to the acronym formed by the three commands: "A-S-K" ("Ask, Seek, Knock"). Remembering each word may help you when you make requests of God in prayer. These commands are similar in meaning in that each emphasizes the importance of asking. There are, however, shades of difference in the implications of each command.

Asking implies that God expects us to bring our needs to Him in prayer. If we ask with pure motives to meet genuine needs and if our requests are in God's will, God promises that we will receive. When you ask, consider two questions:

1. Is my request in harmony with God's Word?
2. Is my request helpful to everyone concerned, so far as I know what is most helpful?

Seeking indicates effort in asking. God begins to do what only He can do in answer to prayer as we begin to do what we can do. John Maxwell writes, "Prayer without action is presumption."[3] The term *seek* is also used in Scripture to describe seeking after God Himself. As you seek in prayer, consider:

- Am I only seeking my own desires, or am I seeking to know God more deeply?
- What part would God have me play in response to this petition?

Knocking speaks of the persistence essential to prayer. The commands become more aggressive, moving from simple asking to more intense seeking to even bolder knocking. The Greek tenses of these verbs strengthen the idea of perseverance even more. Jesus literally is saying, "Keep on asking; keep on seeking; keep on knocking." Then He makes a promise, "For everyone who asks receives, and he who seeks finds, and to him who knocks it will be opened" (Luke 11:10).

Jesus does not say, "Everyone who asks receives exactly what he asks for," or "Everyone who seeks finds exactly what she is searching for," or "Those who knock will walk through the same door they've been knocking on." He does say, though, that God will respond to our heartfelt prayer with an answer. As you pray with persistence, consider:

- How is God changing my requests as I pray?
- How is God changing me as I pray?

A HIDDEN COIN

A man was sitting in his recliner when his four-year-old granddaughter walked into the room. He called her over. Leaning forward in his chair, he winked at her and said, "I've got a quarter hidden in one of my hands. If you can find it, you can have it."

His hands were in front of him, clenched tightly. The little girl said, "Granddaddy, I can't see what's in your hands."

"Why don't you try to open my hands?" he suggested.

So she began to pry apart his large hands, finger by finger. With great effort she opened her granddad's left index finger, middle finger, ring finger, pinky, and thumb. When his left hand was open, she looked into his palm. No quarter.

So, she began working on the right hand. After prying each finger open, she discovered the quarter her grandfather had hidden in the palm of his right hand.

Why didn't the granddad just give the little girl the quarter to begin with? Why did he make her go through all of that trouble?

We could generate a number of answers.

- Maybe he enjoyed the fun of playing a game with her.
- Maybe he thought her effort would help her appreciate his gift.
- Maybe he wanted to see if she trusted him to tell her the truth about the coin.
- Maybe he was trying to develop her perseverance.
- Maybe he was teaching her to follow his directions.

But none of those answers gets at his deepest reason: The man hid the coin and revealed it slowly because he wanted his granddaughter to hold his hands.

When Jesus tells us to keep on asking, seeking, and knocking in prayer, it's not because God wants to play games with us. God uses our determination in prayer to work mightily in our lives:

- He is working in prayer to make us more appreciative.
- He is working to teach us to trust Him.
- He is working to strengthen our patience and perseverance.
- He is working to deepen our obedience and discipleship.

Most of all, though, God is working in prayer to keep our hand in His hand. When we ask and keep on asking, when we seek and keep on seeking, and when we knock and keep on knocking, we're growing closer to Him.

SUGGESTED SCRIPTURE READING

Luke 11:5–13

PRAYER GUIDE

Consider how you might *ask*, *seek*, and *knock* in prayer for . . .

- physical provision for people around you and throughout the world.
- wisdom for daily decisions.
- meeting of spiritual needs in your life and the lives of others.
- greater persistence and confidence in prayer.
- opportunities to share the message of Christ with others.

Day 5

In Jesus's Name

If you ask anything in My name, I
will do it. (John 14:14)

There is a fragrance in the name of
Christ that makes every prayer that
bears it acceptable to God.
                    —R. A. Torrey[1]

Jesus's name opens doors.

Several years ago, Michele and I visited the U.S. Army training installation at Fort Benning, near Columbus, Georgia. It was our first time ever on a military base, and we saw fascinating things. We were impressed by the facilities and the young men and women who were training to be well-prepared infantry soldiers.

A noteworthy part of our visit was the level of security we encountered. We stopped at checkpoint after checkpoint as we traveled through the installation. However, at each instance, the armed guards simply waved us through.

Why did they let us pass? Certainly not because of our qualifications. If we had pulled up to the gate and said, "We'd like to drive around for an hour or so," we would not have been allowed to pass.

We were able to enter because we were with an army captain. He had the credentials to take us past the guards and onto the base. At each checkpoint, our friend simply showed his identification, then pointed to us and said, "They're with me." He was our access.

ENTRANCE THROUGH JESUS

In the same way, our access to God comes only through Christ. Jesus said, "I am the way, the truth, and the life. No one comes to the Father except through Me" (John 14:6). Jesus made exclusive claims for Himself. According to His own testimony, Jesus does not merely *show* the way to the Father. He did not come simply to light a path or blaze a trail. He *is* the way to the Father. He did not claim just to *teach* the truth, like the prophets before Him. He *is* the truth. Jesus did not promise only to *give* life. No, He *embodies* abundant eternal life. Moreover, He did not present Himself as one way to the Father, but as the *only* way.

For believers, every aspect of salvation and our resulting spiritual lives depends completely on Jesus. We are saved in His name (Acts 4:12). We receive the Holy Spirit in His name (John 14:26). We are baptized into His church in His name (Acts 2:38). And, in His name, we bring our prayers to the Father. No one comes to God in prayer except through Him.

In John 14, Jesus introduced His disciples to the idea of praying in His name. In an upstairs room in Jerusalem, they gathered around their Master and listened as He made a surprising promise: "Whatever you ask in My name, that I will do, that the Father may be glorified in the Son. If you ask anything in My name, I will do it" (vv. 13–14).

Consider the full impact of the Lord's words for a moment: Whatever we ask in Jesus's name—anything we ask in His name—He pledges to do. Had Jesus said this only once, it would be true for all eternity. But the Bible gives us greater assurance of this truth, because Jesus repeatedly tells believers that He will grant what we ask in His name. Listen to His words:

- "You did not choose Me, but I chose you and appointed you that you should go and bear fruit, and that your fruit should remain, that whatever you ask the Father in My name He may give you" (John 15:16).
- "Most assuredly, I say to you, whatever you ask the Father in My name He will give you. Until now you have asked nothing in My name. Ask, and you will receive, that your joy may be full" (John 16:23b–24).

It's as though Jesus engraved this precious truth indelibly on the pages of Scripture, set it in bold letters, and underscored it with red ink: He will provide His people what we request in His name. That promise is indisputable.

The question remains: What does this mean to us today?

NO MAGIC FORMULA

To understand what it means to pray in Jesus's name, we must first chase away any false idea that Jesus meant His name to be used as a magical incantation. Some Christians mistakenly and idolatrously treat the Lord's name as an amulet or a good-luck charm.

I know of one pastor who encouraged his congregation to spend an hour simply saying the Lord's name over and over, claiming that there was some mystical power in doing so. While the name of Jesus is indeed the most wonderful name we can pronounce, in whatever language we may speak it, to ascribe magical virtue to the name's use or repetition in prayer violates the command the Lord Himself gave us: "When you pray, do not use vain repetitions as the heathen do. For they think that they will be heard for their many words" (Matt. 6:7). Praying in Jesus's name does not mean emptily repeating His name. Saying "Jesus" again and again as a Hindu might repeat a mantra cheapens our view of Christ and our understanding of prayer.

Praying in Jesus's name also does not mean invoking *His* name to get the results *we* desire. Some people misguidedly believe that if they ask God for something and end their prayer with the phrase, *in Jesus's name*, then God is required to grant their request. Like many Christians, I have made it a lifelong habit to end my prayers by saying, "In Jesus's name, Amen." When Jesus instructed us to pray in His name, though, He meant something far deeper than saying those words.

SEEKING HIS PURPOSE

What does it really mean to pray in Jesus's name? It means praying in harmony with His will, His purpose, and His character. God says: "Now this is the confidence that we have in Him, that if we ask anything according to His will, He hears us" (1 John 5:14).

Asking in Jesus's name is much more than slapping His name at the end of our selfish prayers. When we pray in Jesus's name we are joining in His mission, reflecting His character, and expressing His wishes.

When we finish writing a letter, we may sign off with words or phrases like *sincerely, yours truly, with best regards,* or some other closing. I often end my letters by writing,

> In Jesus's name,
> Stephen Rummage

I sign that way because I want everything I do to honor Christ, even down to the letters and cards I write. Signing *In Jesus's name* helps me to check my motives in the letter. I consciously review the letter before putting those words at the end, asking, "Can I honestly say 'in Jesus's name' with the things I've said? Is the subject matter in keeping with His holiness? Is the purpose of my letter aligned with His will?" If I'm not so sure, or answer *no* to any of those questions, I'm not ready to sign that letter "in Jesus's name." I can sign it in my own name, but not His.

Imagine what it would be like to receive an angry, abusive letter— a letter that ripped you up one side and down the other—signed *In*

Jesus's name. Such a closing would be ridiculous. The letter pretends to be in Jesus's name, but it really isn't.

Praying our own wishes and desires, and then ending the prayer *In Jesus's name, Amen,* is much the same. No one can pray for personal revenge, worldly ambition, or some other unworthy thing *in the name of Jesus.* Though we may presume to be asking in His name, we're actually praying in our own name, according to our own desires, rather than His. Praying in Jesus's name requires asking for the things He would ask for and seeking His purpose.

THE POWER OF HIS NAME

Praying in Jesus's name brings our requests to God under Christ's authority. In the biblical world, a name represented the character and quality of the person who bore that name. To pray in Jesus's name means that we are claiming His authority as the Son of God and Savior. We are coming to God based on Christ's merits, not ours. We can pray with full confidence in the power of Jesus Christ.

The evangelist Billy Sunday once said, "There are two hundred and fifty-six names given in the Bible for the Lord Jesus Christ, and I suppose this was because He was infinitely beyond all that any one name could express." Each title the Bible gives to Jesus reveals a different facet of His holy character. Consider some of the names given to Jesus:

- He is the *Author and Finisher of our Faith* (Heb. 12:2).
- He is the *Beloved* (Eph. 1:6), the *Bridegroom* (John 3:29; Rev. 21:9), and the *Bright and Morning Star* (Rev. 22:16).
- He is the *Chief Cornerstone* (Ps. 118:22) and *Chief Shepherd* (1 Peter 5:4).
- He is *Jesus Christ our Savior* (Titus 3:6), our *Deliverer* (Rom. 11:26), our *Mediator* (1 Tim. 2:5), and our *Advocate* (1 John 2:1).
- He was God's *Messiah* or *Anointed One (*John 4:25–26) to be our *Redeemer* (Isa. 59:20).

- He is *True God* and *Eternal Life* (1 John 5:20), *Everlasting Father* (Isa. 9:6), *Faithful Witness* (Rev. 1:5), and *Firstborn from the Dead* (Col. 1:18).
- He is *God with Us* (Matt. 1:23), the *Great High Priest* (Heb. 4:14), and the *Head of the Church* (Col. 1:18).
- He is the *Image of the Invisible God* (Col. 1:15), the *Only Begotten of the Father* (John 1:14), and *Only Wise God* (1 Tim. 1:17).
- He is *Judge of the Living and the Dead* (Acts 10:42).
- He is the *King Eternal* (1 Tim. 1:17) and the *King of Glory* (Ps. 24:7).
- He is the *Lamb of God* (John 1:36), the *Lion of the Tribe of Judah* (Rev. 5:5), the *Lily of the Valley* (Song 2:1), and our *Lord* (John 21:7).
- He is the *Man of Sorrows* (Isa. 53:3).
- He is to us the *Power of God* (1 Cor. 1:24) and the *Prince of Peace* (Isa. 9:6).
- He is our *Rock* (1 Cor. 10:4), and our *Resurrection* (John 11:25).
- He is the *Son of God* from eternity (Rom. 1:4) and *Son of Man* in His humanity (Acts 7:56).
- He is the *Teacher from God* (John 3:2) and the *True Vine* (John 15:1).
- He is *God's Unspeakable Gift* (2 Cor. 9:15) for which we give thanks, the *Living Way* to God in His body (Heb. 10:20), and the *Word of God* by whom God created all there is (John 1:1).
- He is *Wonderful* (Isa. 9:6).

In every name given to Jesus in God's Word, some aspect of His being or His power and authority comes to light. Praying in His name means availing ourselves of the full measure of His being. Our prayers are not answered on the ground of our own goodness but because Jesus is worthy and we ask in His name.

The power of Jesus's name in prayer has been compared to the name signed on a check. If you go to a bank and give them a check, signed with your name, you are asking the bank to honor your name. If you have money deposited in the bank, your check will be cashed. If you don't have an account there, your name on the check is meaningless. If, however, you go to a bank with someone else's name signed to the check, you are asking for the money in that person's name.

R. A. Torrey wrote: "When I go to God in prayer, it is like going to the bank of heaven. I have nothing deposited there. I have absolutely no credit there. If I go in my own name, I will get absolutely nothing. But Jesus Christ has unlimited credit in heaven, and He has granted me the privilege of going to the bank with His name on my check."[2]

As we pray in Jesus's name, we come to God totally on the merits of Jesus Christ. We come to God not claiming our own power or privileges but in the name of the One to whom all power and glory is due. Jesus's name gives us complete assurance that we will be heard and answered as we come to the Father in prayer.

HIS GLORY ALONE

Praying in Jesus's name implies that all we have said in prayer has been said for the glory of God. Jesus told His disciples that the reason He would do what they asked in His name was "that the Father may be glorified in the Son" (John 14:13). We have already seen that prayers in Jesus's name must be in harmony with His desires. We must also recognize that Christ's great desire is to bring glory and honor to His Father.

If God's glory is Jesus's desire, it should be our desire as well. Reflecting on this truth, James Montgomery Boice wrote, "We are so filled with the idea that prayer is getting something from God that we rarely consider that prayer is actually a means by which God gets something from us. What He wants from us is glory, a glory that will lead others to trust Him."[3]

Ralph Keiper suffered from limited vision. What most people could see from one hundred feet, he could see at ten. Many times when he was a young man, Ralph complained to God because of his poor eyesight. *Why should I suffer from this,* he wondered, *after all, God could do something about this if He wanted to.*

Ralph prayed about his problem but got no immediate answer. He could not understand why God would delay. He was serving the Lord, even going to seminary to prepare for ministry. He was seeking God. Why was God silent?

One Saturday afternoon while Ralph was studying, the Holy Spirit began to speak to him. For years, Ralph had asked God questions in prayer. Now, God was asking him some questions.

He sensed the Spirit asking, "Ralph, what is the chief end of man?"

Ralph gave the *Westminster Shorter Catechism's* classic answer, "To glorify God, and to enjoy Him forever!"

"Do you wish to glorify God?"

"Of course!" That answer came easily.

"Ralph, if you had the choice, what would you rather do, glorify God or have perfect vision?"

Ralph paused. He had to be honest because the Holy Spirit was watching.

"There is only one answer," he said finally, "and that is to glorify God."

"Do you really believe that God's glory is more important than your vision?"

"My vision, or lack of it, is not worthy to be compared to the glory of God!"

"Do you really wish to glorify God?" the Holy Spirit asked again.

"Yes, I do!" Ralph said in surrender.

"If you do, why worry about the method God chooses for you to glorify Him?"[4]

When we pray in Jesus's name in the fullest sense, it brings us to the place of seeking God's glory alone—above our own desires, even beyond our own apparent needs. Jesus's name compels us to ask those things that bring about God's glory and honor. And here's the beauty of it: Jesus promised that every prayer offered in His name that seeks His Father's glory will receive the answer *yes*!

SUGGESTED SCRIPTURE READING

Romans 11:33–36

PRAYER GUIDE

Thoughtfully petition God in Jesus's name, reflecting on these questions:

- Is this the kind of prayer that Jesus wants me to pray?
- Is Jesus honored by my requests?
- Am I praying what I believe to be the will of Christ?
- Am I willing for God to be glorified in my life, even at the cost of my greatest desires?

Day 6

NOT AS I WILL,
BUT AS YOU WILL

He went a little farther and fell on
His face, and prayed, saying, "O My
Father, if it is possible, let this cup
pass from Me; nevertheless, not as I
will, but as You will." (Matt. 26:39)

I cannot pray in the name of Jesus
to have my own will.
—Søren Kierkegaard[1]

*A*uthentic prayer produces surrender.

A fundamental of water safety is never to attempt to rescue a man
from drowning while he's still trying to save himself. If a drowning
man is fighting to keep himself afloat, he is deadly to anyone who
tries to help. In his effort to keep from going under, he will grab the
person trying to rescue him, and both of them will go down.

So, instead of struggling with a drowning man, the rescuer should
first swim near the person but stay out of arm's reach. And then, the
rescuer should wait. Though it may be difficult to watch the person

struggle, trying to help could be suicide. Only when the man gives up does the rescuer move in, for then the drowning man is compliant. He won't work against the savior.

GIVE UP?

Charles Stanley compares a drowning man surrendering to the believer's surrender to God, writing, "Until we give up, we aren't really in a position to be helped. We will work against Him rather than with Him. Surrender to His will follows the surrender of our own."[2]

Nineteenth-century preacher Joseph Parker wrote that "prayers are battles." An epic struggle ensues as the believer prays.

The battle in genuine prayer is never the struggle to bring God into line with our plans. Some Christians misguidedly believe that if they repeatedly pray for the wishes of their hearts, God eventually will acquiesce. They keep praying, "God, give me a nicer house," or "God, grant me this promotion," or "God, give me an A in this course," or "God, make this person agreeable to marrying me," without truly considering God's plan for them.

The great conflict in prayer is the battle to relinquish the human will. God works in prayer to bring us to a place of trust, obedience, and surrender to His purpose. When you pray, the voice of God is telling you, *"Give up. Let me take over."*

In Matthew 26, the Bible records a prayer Jesus prayed the night before He was crucified. In Christ's prayer in Gethsemane, we witness the painful but beautiful expression of a heart totally abandoned to God, one willing to do what God wants no matter what the cost. From this prayer, believers can learn profound lessons about surrender through prayer.

DEEP SORROW IN THE GARDEN

East of the temple and across the River Kidron is the garden of Gethsemane. The garden gets its name from the Aramaic term for "oil press." That name, along with the garden's location on the Mount of Olives, has led many students of the Bible to believe that the spot was full of olive trees. Probably during His visits to Jerusalem, Jesus had lingered many hours praying by those trees, since Judas seems to have known that Jesus could be found there. Matthew reports what happened during the Lord's last visit there:

> Then Jesus came with them to a place called Gethsemane, and said to the disciples, "Sit here while I go and pray over there." And He took with Him Peter and the two sons of Zebedee, and He began to be sorrowful and deeply distressed. Then He said to them, "My soul is exceedingly sorrowful, even to death. Stay here and watch with Me." (Matt. 26:36–38)

Perhaps Gethsemane was the property of friends who invited the Lord to rest and pray in their garden. On other occasions, the Lord might have spent joyful times there, communing with His Father. Tonight, though, was different. After leaving eight of the disciples at the entrance, Jesus took Peter, James, and John farther in. These three disciples—who had been eyewitnesses to Jesus's miracles, who had listened as He proclaimed the good news of God's kingdom, and who had even glimpsed His transfigured glory—now saw the deepest sorrow etched on their Master's face.

The words the Bible uses to describe Jesus's emotional and mental state in Gethsemane are especially moving: "He began to be sorrowful and deeply distressed" (Matt. 26:37b). *Deeply distressed* speaks of being loaded down with a great heaviness. With each step, Jesus anticipated the weight of the crossbeam that would soon be fastened to His shoulders. But, far worse, He awaited the incalculable burden of human wickedness that would press down on His body as He provided payment for sin. The Lord's spirit was heavy as He prayed.

Matthew describes Jesus as being sorrowful, but Christ Himself used an even more severe expression, saying, "My soul is exceedingly sorrowful, even to death" (Matt. 26:38a). *Exceedingly sorrowful* speaks of the enormity of His grief. In the original language, Jesus used a single term that has two components: *grieved* and *around*. The combination of the two ideas paints a picture of someone who is suffering on every side. There is sorrow from within and without, from the left and the right, from above and below. In every direction He faced, Jesus experienced grief and sorrow.

The chilling breath of agony blew upon Jesus's soul as He prayed. His soul was grieved "to death," Jesus said. Intense anguish was crushing the life out of Him. No one wants to die at age thirty-three, nor would any man or woman desire to suffer the torture of crucifixion. But we must not think that it was primarily the fear of death or physical pain that encompassed the Lord with distress and grief in the garden. The sorrow He felt was driven by the unspeakable horror of His pure heart as He anticipated becoming a sin offering for us. Sinful men and women cannot conceive what it meant to Him, the sinless Son of God, to become sin for us. That destiny loomed in front of Jesus.

YOUR GETHSEMANE

Christians who lead lives of prayer can know a version of the Gethsemane experience. Our pain cannot be compared to the agony Christ endured, but we will feel the anguish of grief pressing from every side. To follow Christ in prayer is to share in that kind of sorrow.

My office phone rang. As soon as I heard Tim's voice, I could detect the stress in his tone.

"We've experienced a tragedy," he said.

Tim is pastor of a church in eastern North Carolina and a model of absolute trust in God through every issue in his life. He's the kind of man who prays at every opportunity. He and I have prayed together in the pastor's study of his church, in his car, in seminary classrooms, and in restaurants. He lives by prayer.

"What's going on?" I asked.

Tim and his brother married sisters. Tim and his wife lived next door to his brother's family. The two couples had three children each, and all their kids were raised together. Now Tim's oldest nephew had been killed in an automobile accident, and Tim felt just as devastated as if he had lost his own son. When a young man dies, hopes and dreams and aspirations and potential seem to die with him.

"I've always preached about trust and confidence in the Lord," he said, "and I believe what I said. But it's hard when you have to go through times like this."

Tim and I prayed together, knowing that God was somehow working even in this time of desolation. Here were the shadows of Gethsemane. Every Christian will experience hard times of heaviness, distress, and extreme sorrow. How will we respond? Jesus shows us that the best response is the prayer of surrender.

A RELINQUISHED HEART

After instructing Peter, James, and John to watch with Him, Jesus went deeper into the garden. There in the darkness, He poured out His heart to God in agonized prayer.

A diamond is often displayed against a black backdrop. The luster is more striking in contrast to the darkness surrounding it. In the blackness of Gethsemane, the radiance of the Lord's heart shone brightly. Here's the sparkling beauty of this anguished time in Jesus's life: In spite of His sorrow and distress, knowing the suffering He would experience in the coming hours, Jesus surrendered His will to the Father's. Listen to His words as He yielded to the Father's purposes: "O My Father, if it is possible, let this cup pass from Me; nevertheless, not as I will, but as You will" (Matt. 26:39b).

Mark's account of this story tells us that Jesus began His prayer by saying, "Abba, Father, all things are possible for You" (Mark 14:36). *Abba* was the Aramaic equivalent of "Daddy" or "Papa." Jesus used the same term of tenderness and dependence for His Father that a small child would use. He recognized the power and sovereignty His Father possessed. Even as He surrendered, Jesus understood that it was within God's ability to provide escape. Yet, He relinquished His own heart, praying, "Not as I will, but as You will."

Jesus was saying, "Father, let Your will happen in My life." He was distraught at the prospect of taking sin upon Himself. Yet He was willing to drink the cup of suffering to its dregs to obey the will of His Father. Meekly and submissively, Jesus was surrendering to whatever answer God sent. Richard Foster writes, "To applaud the will of God, to do the will of God, even to fight for the will of God is not difficult . . . until it comes at cross-purposes with our will. Then the lines are drawn."[3] Jesus was at a crossroads where His preferences differed from the Father's plan. Through prayer, He adjusted His desires to align with the Father's will.

Christ's surrender in the garden of Gethsemane prepared Him for the path He had to walk. Each step to Golgotha was a step of obedience. The words Jesus spoke to His disciples after praying show that the Lord was ready to go to the cross: "Behold, the hour is at hand, and the Son of Man is being betrayed into the hands of sinners. Rise, let us be going. See, My betrayer is at hand" (Matt. 26:45b–46).

"Let us be going," Jesus said. Those were not words of retreat but a command to enter the heat of battle. Fully surrendered to His Father, Christ was now ready to endure whatever suffering awaited Him. In the events that followed—His betrayal and arrest, His trial, His scourging and mockery, and His crucifixion—there was never hesitation in the Lord's steps, because Jesus had already exchanged His will for God's.

Reflecting on the implications of the Lord's surrender, the Scottish preacher and poet George Matheson wrote: "The cup which our Father giveth us to drink is a cup for the will. It is easy for the lips to drain it when once the heart has accepted it. Not on the heights of Calvary, but in the shadows of Gethsemane is the cup presented; the act is easy after the choice." Matheson's beautiful hymn, "Make Me a Captive, Lord," expresses the same thought:

> Make me a captive, Lord,
> And then I shall be free.
> Force me to render up my sword,
> And I shall conqueror be.

> I sink in life's alarms
> When by myself I stand;
> Imprison me within thine arms,
> And strong shall be my hand.
> (George Matheson, "Make Me a
> Captive, Lord," 1890)

One man hung a sign in his room that expresses the daily prayer of his heart. He reads that little sign first thing every morning, right after he wakes up. Here's what it says: "What have You got going today, God? I'd like to be a part of it." That may seem like a simple prayer, but surrender is as uncomplicated as it is difficult. The practical outworking of surrender is signing your name at the bottom of God's blank page, and saying, "Whatever You want, Lord." God desires us to surrender to Him daily, and He accomplishes that surrender through prayer.

WATCH AND PRAY

There's another aspect to the story of Christ's prayer in the garden. We've touched its outer edges, but we need to consider it more deeply, because it pertains directly to us. Jesus had brought three men—His most intimate friends—to pray with Him. The Lord came to check on them three times; on each occasion, He found them sleeping. The drama of the last few days and hours had drained them to the point that they could not keep from falling asleep, even in those crucial moments.

We find it hard to imagine that Jesus's closest disciples would be so careless as to fall asleep three times in the garden. After all, He only asked for them to pray an hour, and they surely had some idea of how critical this hour was for the Lord. With the insight of a physician, Luke reports that they were sleeping "from sorrow" (Luke 22:45). Perhaps sleep overcame the men because they could not bear to think about the pain their Lord would soon endure. Still, we wonder, how could they have fallen asleep at a time like that?

Any criticism we might raise vanishes, though, when we consider how many times we have fallen asleep praying, or how often our minds have wandered when we should have been watching. The disciples' weakness in prayer was all too human, and Jesus's response to them speaks to us today. "Then He came to the disciples and found them sleeping, and said to Peter, 'What? Could you not watch with Me one hour? Watch and pray, lest you enter into temptation. The spirit indeed is willing, but the flesh is weak'" (Matt. 26:40–41).

The Lord's instructions to them were clear and simple: *Watch and pray.* Jesus knew the struggle He was having within Himself. He knew that His disciples also faced temptations to follow their own desires rather than surrender to God's will. Jesus commanded them to watch and pray not to shame them but to give them strength. *Watch* is a term that suggests a soldier on guard. Jesus was saying, "Be on your guard!" The temptation to go your own way rather than God's way is all too real. The command to *pray* points to the way Jesus Himself was praying—seeking strength to submit to God in the face of inward apprehension.

THE PRICE OF SURRENDER

Walking along a city sidewalk, you may pause to look at the display in a store window. Expensive watches or earrings or fine clothing on display catch your eye. But as you admire the items for sale, you know that the prices are more than you are willing to pay. Methodist missionary E. Stanley Jones said, "If you make a compromise with surrender, you can remain interested in the abundant life, all the riches of freedom, love, and peace, but it is the same as looking at a display in a shop window. You look through the window but do not go in and buy. You will not pay the price—surrender."[4]

Surrender is the price for God's purpose in your life. It's a high price. Amazingly and graciously, though, God uses the struggle of prayer to strengthen our trust in Him so that we can surrender.

SUGGESTED SCRIPTURE READING

Isaiah 53:1–7; 64:8

PRAYER GUIDE

As you seek a relinquished heart, ask God . . .

- that as Jesus was surrendered to God's purpose for Him, you will be surrendered.
- that God will make your life like clay in His loving hands.
- that God will grant you grace to exchange your will for His, even when His plan involves sorrow, pain, or what the world would consider failure.

Day 7

PRAYING IN JESUS'S FOOTSTEPS

A pastor visited a member of his congregation in a psychiatric hospital many years ago. While the minister was there, one of the hospital administrators took him on a brief tour of the facility.

This was in the time when several patients might share an open ward, and as they passed one such ward, the administrator pointed out a powerfully built young man. The pastor noted how strong the young man looked and asked, "If he had a psychotic break, would a patient like that be difficult to control?"

"Yes," said the administrator, "but that won't happen. A symptom of this man's condition is that he perceives that he has no strength at all. He's always asking for medicine and complaining that he is weak."

Believers suffer from a similar spiritual delusion. We fail to realize the real power for living that we have through prayer. When we follow in Jesus's footsteps, we find that His is the pathway of prayer.

In Jesus's practice and teaching on prayer, we observed that, through Christ's power, we can have a surrendered prayer life. We can present our requests to God in Jesus's name, knowing that God will hear and answer. He also will enable us to make time in our busiest schedules to seek Him.

SUGGESTED SCRIPTURE READING

Hebrews 4:14–16

PRAYER GUIDE

As you pray, praise Jesus for:

- His life of prayer and victory over sin.
- His teaching and example of prayer.
- His death on the cross that offers access to God.
- His promise to always make intercession for His people.
- His grace that enables endurance in times of need.
- His assurance that He is coming again.

Part 2

HANNAH'S PRAYER OF DESPERATION

Principles for Praying with Purpose
God knows your burdens.
God cares about you.
God remembers your prayers.
Praise adorns genuine prayer.
Prayer acknowledges God's sovereignty.

Day 8

High Hopes and Deep Needs

As a woman, I have always valued great heroines of the faith—to follow, respect, and pattern my life after. Throughout our lives, Stephen and I have been blessed by the prayers and examples of such women.

On many mornings during college, Stephen became aware as he woke up that his mother's hand was gently resting on his forehead. She was praying for him before she left home for her daily activities. I can remember hearing my own mother call my name in prayer many times as I was growing up. In our years of ministry together, Stephen and I have listened with joy as godly women poured out their hearts to God in church prayer gatherings. We have enlisted the prayers of homebound widows who are great prayer warriors to intercede for the souls of men and women our church was trying to reach for Christ. Listening to these women, both Stephen and I have learned more about how to pray.

When I study my Bible, I find a woman who holds the standard high in devotion to God in the midst of great pain. I have learned some of my life's most precious lessons in prayer from her. Her name was Hannah. Hannah's desperate prayer for a son and the song of praise Hannah offered when the Lord provided Samuel offers a beautiful example of how to bring our hopes and needs to God. Whether

Hannah's faith in God grew strong because of her infertility or in spite of it, she was a woman who trusted God with all her being.

Hannah is portrayed as a pious woman. She is the only woman that the Old Testament shows going up to the Lord's house and the only woman who is shown making and fulfilling a vow to the Lord. Hannah is the only woman in the Old Testament who is specifically shown in prayer. Hers is among the longest recorded prayers in the historical account of Israel. Possibly because we have her lengthy prayer, she is heard calling on *Yahweh* more specifically and more often than any other woman we meet before Mary the mother of Jesus. It's no wonder that Hannah called on the Lord's name so profusely. She had a great faith, high hopes, and deep needs.

Childlessness was considered a curse. To make matters worse, her husband had taken another wife, who made life miserable for Hannah. Yet, she offered her broken heart to God in prayer, and the Lord answered with grace, love, power, and compassion.

Most of us have experienced the disappointment of frustrated hopes, whether our hope was for a job, a relationship, a child, or a physical problem. From Hannah, we learn how to turn our sorrows into prayers of faith to the Lord.

SUGGESTED SCRIPTURE READING

1 Samuel 1:1–2:11

PRAYER GUIDE

As you pray,

- thank God that He knows how to provide for all your needs.
- ask for His protection against bitterness or frustration when life does not go the way you had hoped.

- ask Him to teach you to trust Him through Hannah's example.
- ask that the Lord give you love and compassion for those whose hearts are burdened by needs in their lives.

Day 9

Praying Through Pain

The LORD had closed her womb.
(1 Sam. 1:5b)

God whispers to us in our pleasures, speaks in our conscience, but
shouts in our pains: it is His mega-
phone to rouse a deaf world.
—C. S. Lewis[1]

God knows your burdens.

A man was carrying a sack of grain down a country road. His
worn shirt was covered with sweat. The noon sun was beating down
on the weary man. The driver of a passing wagon noticed this struggle, and—judging the sack to weigh at least fifty pounds—he gently
tugged on the reins to stop his team.

"Mister, you need a ride. Get up here with me, and I'll take you."

Relieved, the tired man climbed up onto the seat and settled in for
the remainder of the trip to town. But he never removed the loaded
sack from his shoulder. He continued carrying it as he rode.

After a moment of silence, the driver asked, "Why don't you put
that sack down and relax?"

"Oh no!" the man replied. "It's enough to ask you to carry me without also carrying this heavy load."[2]

Have you ever had such an attitude with God? As believers in Christ, we have entrusted our souls to Him. We have come to Him by faith, saying, "Lord, I am counting on You to cleanse me of my sin, to bring me into Your family, and to grant me eternal life through Jesus. I am giving You my soul, Lord."

Why, then, would we hesitate to give Him our cares, worries, needs, and burdens? If He is able to save us, He surely is able to meet our deepest needs. God tells us, "Cast your burden on the LORD, and He shall sustain you" (Ps. 55:22a). He wants to ease your burdens and carry your heavy load.

Through faith in Him, you can pray through your pain.

HEARTBROKEN HANNAH

At the beginning of 1 Samuel, God's Word introduces us to a woman named Hannah. She lived in Israel near the end of the era of the judges. These judges were national heroes—men and women God raised up to deliver His people from danger and guide them. Hannah would become the mother of Samuel—the last great judge of Israel and the first kingdom prophet. In fact, God used Samuel to anoint the first two kings of Israel.

As 1 Samuel opens, though, such a birth is nothing more than a dream for Hannah. We meet her as a brokenhearted woman, because Hannah has not been able to have a child.

The unfulfilled yearning for a baby to hold, nurture, and love is a source of sorrow for many women, as it has been throughout history. In Scripture we meet a number of women with fertility problems, among them Sarah, Rebekah, Rachel, and Elizabeth. Among the Jews, a woman's inability to have children was considered a sign of God's displeasure. Hannah came to God in prayer with a broken heart and a deep need.

Maybe your deepest need isn't a child, but God cares about your heartaches. Whatever your needs are, God knows them, and He is able to meet them. He understands where you hurt the most, and He invites you to bring your longings to Him in prayer.

MEETING GOD

At the beginning of Hannah's story, we see the family struggles and inner turmoil that moved her to seek God in prayer. Hannah was married to a man named Elkanah. We know little about Elkanah except that he was committed to God. A member of the priestly line, he took his family each year to worship and offer sacrifices to the Lord at the tabernacle in Shiloh (1 Sam. 1:3). Elkanah's home in the region of Ephraim was at least fifteen miles from Shiloh. It was a lengthy trip to make on foot even once a year, but they took the time and gave the energy to meet with God.[3]

The diligence shown by Elkanah, Hannah, and the rest of the family raises immediate questions when we evaluate our own lives:

- How dedicated are we to meet with God?
- How much effort will we expend to come to God's house to worship Him?
- How often do we meet with God in prayer, when we can call on Him anywhere we are?

How easily we become distracted in our devotional lives. Sometimes we won't turn off the television, put down the newspaper, or get out of the bed to meet with God. We let things like the weather or the sniffles keep us from church, when we would never let such inconsequential things keep us from work or school. Are you willing to "go the distance" to meet with God? If you are truly interested in bringing your prayers to the Lord, you'll make the effort to meet with Him each day.

Scottish preacher Robert Murray M'Cheyne died at the age of thirty. In his brief career, though, his life burned brightly for Christ. A hunger for God drove him to his knees. His desire to know God and to meet with Him is evident in a journal entry for one Sabbath day in February: "Rose early to seek God, and found Him whom my soul loveth. Who would not rise early to meet such company?"[4]

M'Cheyne's time of prayer was more than a routine; it was his source of daily spiritual life. His time of communion with the Father was not a chore but a joy—because he knew that God met with him in those special times. So it was with Hannah as she went to Shiloh. She was expecting and desiring to meet with God.

FAMILY CONFLICT

Hannah carried the burden of a fractured family. Although Elkanah loved Hannah and although he led his family to worship the Lord, there was a great conflict in this man's household. The problem was Elkanah's own foolish decision: "And he had two wives: the name of one was Hannah, and the name of the other Peninnah. Peninnah had children, but Hannah had no children. . . . And her rival also provoked her severely, to make her miserable, because the LORD had closed her womb" (1 Sam. 1:2, 6).

Elkanah—like the patriarchs Abraham, Isaac, and Jacob—had a first wife who was barren. So that he might produce an heir, Elkanah took an additional wife. When Elkanah took Peninnah as his second wife, he was following cultural practice, but polygamy had always been an act of disobedience to God's plan. Upon instituting marriage in the garden of Eden, God had said, "Therefore a man shall leave his father and mother and be joined to his wife, and they shall become one flesh" (Gen. 2:24). God never intended for a man to have more than one wife. Elkanah did things his way instead of God's way. God says, "There is a way that seems right to a man, but its end is the way of death" (Prov. 14:12). God's way is always best. When we depart from His way, we miss out on His best.

That's what happened in Elkanah's household. In a home that should have been filled with the peace of God, there was great discord. We can only imagine Hannah's pain at having to share her home with Peninnah. To watch Peninnah present newborn babies to her husband only compounded Hannah's misery.

Hannah was not the only one hurt by this arrangement. Peninnah saw that her husband loved Hannah more. Her emotional pain encouraged the jealousy that caused her to taunt and make fun of Hannah for being childless. Maybe Peninnah thought she would win her husband's undivided attention by mocking Hannah.

The Bible paints a picture of constant turmoil: "So it was, year by year, when she went up to the house of the LORD, that she [Peninnah] provoked her [Hannah]" (1 Sam. 1:7a). Peninnah wanted nothing more than to break Hannah's heart. She found delight in causing Hannah to grieve and weep.

Consider the character and the emotions of Hannah and Peninnah as they made the long journey to Shiloh each year:

- *Peninnah*—feeling unloved by her husband, likely burning with bitterness toward him and definitely showing hatred for Hannah. As Peninnah went to God's tabernacle—supposedly to worship—her hands were stained by her deliberate and habitual sin against Hannah.
- *Hannah*—weighed down by the problems in her home, but desperately hoping for deliverance by the hand of the Lord.

Now, consider how you come to God in prayer and worship. Have you ever tried to praise Him with a dirty, sin-stained heart? We should not be surprised that we get nothing out of worship when our lives are in that condition. To worship God fully, we come before Him with holy hands and a pure heart.

Or, as Hannah, have you ever come to prayer feeling the heaviness of personal problems and seeking God's solution? Burdened in her heart, Hannah brought her feuding and dysfunctional family to God in prayer. She would find in God all that she needed, and so will we.

Many homes are places of sorrow and misery rather than havens of joy. This is true even among Christian families. Conflict and distress can come from a number of sources. A home can be disrupted by the death of a spouse or child. Husbands and wives clash with one another. Children and parents can't communicate. Families suffer when there is the furor of a divorce. After a divorce, men and women try to find happiness in remarriage and endure another struggle as two families try to blend together.

Prayer can transform our homes. As we pray for our families, there are two requests that God will always honor:

First, we can ask for greater love for our families. We need to ask God to help us love the other people in our homes in the ways God loves them and loves us. Jesus said, "A new commandment I give to you, that you love one another; as I have loved you, that you also love one another" (John 13:34).

God wants us to love each other, no matter what happens in our families. God's Word tells us, "In sincere love of the brethren, love one another fervently with a pure heart" (1 Peter 1:22b). Sometimes we have conflict at home simply because we don't love each other with a pure heart. Gods wants us to seek each other's best, putting the other person's needs first. If we begin to love one another as God commanded, what a difference there will be.

Second, we can ask for a forgiving spirit in our families. God has commanded us to forgive (Col. 3:13). Sometimes in our marriages, we want to win the fight or be right so badly that we don't care what God says. A wife may say, "He hurt me so deeply that I can't forgive him." A husband may think, "She said such a hateful thing that I can't forget it." Too frequently we hold on to our hurts and disappointments so we can use them for ammunition in an argument. Parents, children, and spouses are tempted to file away the failures of others so we can throw the hurt back into the offender's face at an opportune time. We want to hurt them like they hurt us.

But God calls us to be renewed by having loving and forgiving hearts. Ask yourself, "How many times has God loved and forgiven me? How many hurtful and hateful things have I said to others and God, and yet God still forgave me when I asked?" The psalmist writes, "As far as the east is from the west, so far has He removed our transgressions from us" (Ps. 103:12). God can change our bitter and hurtful hearts into His loving and forgiving heart, if we only ask.

GOD'S PLAN

As Hannah came before the Lord in the tabernacle in Shiloh, she also was struggling with the reality of God's plan for her life. She knew the power of God enough to discern that her infertility had more than a physical cause. Her inability to bear children was a work of the Lord: "The LORD had closed her womb" (1 Sam. 1:5b).

Why would the Lord do something like this to Hannah? After all, God had commanded His people to be fruitful and multiply. That was the first recorded commandment the Lord gave to humankind (Gen. 1:28). In the case of Hannah, we can read ahead to know that God was going to open her womb and bring baby Samuel into the world. We know what a crucial role Hannah's son would play in the history of God's people, Israel.

So, why would God cause a delay in giving a child to Hannah? We might suggest several reasons:

- *The Lord was forcing Hannah to come closer to Him.* Year after year she learned to rely on Him as she brought this need before God.
- *Her burden made Hannah a stronger woman of faith.* After experiencing God's miraculous answer to an impossible situation, Hannah's trust in God would remain deep.
- *Hannah's desperation contributed to the molding of Samuel's character.* Because Hannah gave birth to Samuel, she dedicated her little boy to the Lord, as she probably would not have in normal circumstances. This child was nurtured by both his mother and the high priest for his task as a prophet and judge.

Whatever the full extent of His reasons, God delayed in giving Hannah a son because it was His plan. We may not always know why God is doing what He's doing. But we can always trust that His plans are the best. He says, "I know the thoughts that I think toward you, says the LORD, thoughts of peace and not of evil, to give you a future and a hope. Then you will call upon Me and go and pray to Me, and I will listen to you. And you will seek Me and find Me, when you search for Me with all your heart" (Jer. 29:11–13). The struggles we face will either draw us to God or away from Him. As we trust God with our burdens, He will use them to make us strong men and women of faith and prayer.

JESUS CAN HELP ME

During the nineteenth century, Elisha A. Hoffman served for thirty-three years as pastor of the Benton Harbor Presbyterian Church in Pennsylvania. Widowed at a young age, he was a gifted counselor, the kind of man who could help people trust God with their hurts.

One day Hoffman was ministering to an impoverished community in Lebanon, Pennsylvania. There, he visited a woman whose depression seemed beyond cure. The lady opened her heart and poured out all her pent-up sorrows.

Wringing her hands, she cried, "What shall I do? Oh, what shall I do?"

Hoffman had himself learned the deeper lessons of God's comfort. He said to the woman, "You cannot do better than to take all your sorrows to Jesus. You must tell Jesus."

Suddenly the lady's face lighted up. "Yes!" she cried, "That's it! I must tell Jesus."[5]

Her words echoed in Hoffman's ears. He returned home to use these words as the basis for a song that has blessed many Christians:

> I must tell Jesus! I must tell Jesus!
> I cannot bear my burdens alone;
> I must tell Jesus! I must tell Jesus!
> Jesus can help me, Jesus alone.
> ("I Must Tell Jesus," 1893)

When you pray, bring your burdens to the Lord. He can help!

SUGGESTED SCRIPTURE READING

John 15:9–17

PRAYER GUIDE

As you pray,

- ask God for His love to abide in you.
- ask God for His love so you can forgive.
- ask God for His love so you can love others as He commanded.
- ask God for His love to flow through you so you can bear fruit.
- praise God for His love and forgiveness.

FALLING INTO GOD'S ARMS

And she was in bitterness of soul,
and prayed to the LORD and wept in
anguish. (1 Sam. 1:10)

When life knocks you to your
knees—well, that's the best position
in which to pray, isn't it?
—Ethel Barrymore[1]

God cares about you.

Early one fall, while the leaves were still on the trees, an exceptionally heavy snowstorm suddenly came through. When the streets were clear and the snow had begun to melt, a woman took her grandson on a drive to see the landscape.

"Look at those elms," she said as they passed by a city park. "The branches are so badly broken that the trees may die."

A little farther down the street, they saw a cluster of pine trees. They were bent over—some of them bowed close to the ground—but none of them were broken.

"Grandmommy," the boy asked, "why are those tree bent over?"

"Because the pine trees are wiser than the elms," she answered.

"An elm tree holds its branches rigid. When it becomes weighted down, the limbs eventually break. But when a pine tree is loaded down, it lowers its branches and lets the weight slip away."

Believers who give all their cares to the Lord can face life's burdens much better than those who try to carry the weight themselves.

Perhaps you're a caregiver—a teacher, a nurse, or a counselor. Maybe you're a mother with small children or the spouse of an invalid. Or maybe you have elderly parents who increasingly depend on you. You have your own struggles, disappointments, and heartaches. You may wonder sometimes if anyone cares about you. God does. He knows your sorrow as no one else does, and He understands the depths of your misery. He is waiting for you to give Him the cares of your life.

Today, we're going to look at the way Hannah gave the weight of her sorrow to the Lord. Just as those pine trees bent down to the ground, Hannah bowed before the Lord, and trusted Him with her cares. As Hannah prayed, she discovered how deeply God cared about her.

BEARING ONE ANOTHER'S BURDENS

"Bear one another's burdens, and so fulfill the law of Christ" (Gal. 6:2). One of the ways that God shows His love for us is by placing caring people in our lives. In our churches, in our communities, and especially in our marriages and homes, God uses our human relationships to provide encouragement and help in our times of need.

Hannah's husband, Elkanah, saw her sorrow over being unable to have children. Though Hannah never responded to the unkind remarks, Elkanah noticed the hurt when Peninnah made fun of her. He could see the redness in her eyes and the tears that streaked her cheeks. He had given Hannah a double portion of the offering meal at the tabernacle in Shiloh, only to watch her sit silently at the dinner table. She didn't take a bite of her food as the rest of the family ate and drank.

Because he loved Hannah deeply and saw her grief, Elkanah was grieved too. "Hannah, why do you weep?" he asked with a tender voice. "Why do you not eat? And why is your heart grieved? Am I not better to you than ten sons?" (1 Sam. 1:8).

Elkanah shared in Hannah's trouble and despair. The marital relationship is one of love and respect, of caring and devotion. Elkanah exemplified the words of instruction that Paul would write centuries later: "Husbands ought to love their own wives as their own bodies; he who loves his wife loves himself" (Eph. 5:28). Elkanah loved his wife as his own body. When she hurt, he hurt.

Ultimately, God wants believers to bring our burdens to Him. He invites us to cast all our cares upon Him, knowing that He cares for us (1 Peter 5:7). "Cast your burden on the LORD," wrote the psalmist, "and He shall sustain you" (Ps. 55:22a). But God also wants us to share our burdens with each other. He has told us in His Word: "Confess your trespasses to one another, and pray for one another, that you may be healed" (James 5:16a). "Rejoice with those who rejoice, and weep with those who weep" (Rom. 12:15).

Are we caring for one another in our marriage relationships, in our homes, and within the fellowship of our church? Here are some practical ways we can bear one another's burdens.

- *Be there.* Sometimes the greatest aid we can give a hurting person is the ministry of presence. Simply by being beside a person in a time of need, God can use us.
- *Ask questions.* We should not hesitate to ask hurting people about their needs, not to pry but so that we can minister to them.
- *Offer yourself.* Hurting people need to know that those who care about them are available to help in practical ways.
- *Pray.* When someone is hurting, take every opportunity to pray for that person. When they share their need with you, pray with them, at that moment if possible.

THE CRY OF A TROUBLED HEART

After her family had finished eating, Hannah found a quiet place in the tabernacle and began to pour out a tearful prayer to the Lord. "And she was in bitterness of soul, and prayed to the LORD and wept in anguish" (1 Sam. 1:10). With her knees bent and her face bowed low, Hannah cried out to God with a broken heart. She was crumpled on the floor, praying in agony.

The world is full of people with troubled hearts. A boy with an underdeveloped arm is mocked by his classmates. A widow recalls the pain of the day her husband committed suicide. A mother and father grieve over a wayward son. A man lovingly cares for his wife, who has Alzheimer's disease and no longer recognizes him. A wife weeps over her husband's infidelity.

God hears the cries of troubled hearts.

Hannah prayed to God from the deepest place in her heart. She moved her lips, but no sound came out. Instead, Hannah's true communion with the Lord spoke more loudly than any human voice could ever speak. She understood how holy and powerful God is. She knew God loved and cared for her and her burdens.

Over the years, her grief had driven her to complete trust in Him. She had a praying relationship with her heavenly Father, and she understood that her greatest power was not reflected in her position in society but in her posture before God. She believed God alone had the power to relieve her heartache.

We will bring our heartaches to God only when we realize that He has the power to meet our needs. Often, we may be tempted to let our heartaches lure us away from prayer. We give up praying—maybe because we think God has given up on us. Instead, we should follow the example Jesus set when He prayed in Gethsemane: "And being in agony, He prayed more earnestly" (Luke 22:44a). Jesus's burdens caused Him to pray more, not less.

So it was with Hannah. A heart of longing for God caused her to pray with weeping and a broken heart. She humbled herself on the ground to be as close to her loving Father as she could get.

Do you weep in prayer before holy God? Does your heart break and long for God's loving touch? Only God can take care of your burden. God listens to His children when we weep before Him.

MAKING PROMISES IN PRAYER

"Then she made a vow and said, 'O LORD of hosts, if You will indeed look on the affliction of Your maidservant and remember me, and not forget Your maidservant, but will give Your maidservant a male child, then I will give him to the LORD all the days of his life, and no razor shall come upon his head'" (1 Sam. 1:11). The intensity of Hannah's trust in God and her great longing to have a child moved her to make a binding promise to God. If God would give her a son, she would devote that son to Him.

Hannah knew her position before the Lord. She referred to herself as God's "maidservant," using the term for a common slave. Begging God to look upon her affliction, Hannah pleaded for God's mercy and grace. She asked God to give her a male child, so she could give him back.

Firstborn sons of the Hebrews were presented to the Lord when they were a month old. Since the firstborn was regarded as God's property, it was necessary for the father to redeem or buy back the child from the priest. Hannah made a promise to God that her son would be given to Him. She vowed that "no razor shall come upon his head." Hannah was dedicating her unborn son to God in the strongest way. She was placing the Nazarite vow upon the child, pledging that he would not cut his hair and that he would live in service to God.

Though Hannah was desperate to have children, she did not want a son to keep for herself. She wanted him as a gift to give to her husband and ultimately as a gift to God. If God chose to bless her with a son, Hannah promised that her son would be a blessing to others.

Hannah's promise to God in prayer holds principles for our lives. *First, Hannah reminds us that God gives our children to us.* In some traditions, Christian parents "dedicate" their children to the Lord in a public way. All parents should commit to honor God with our sons and daughters, praying for the day that they will trust Jesus for salvation. We should pledge to help our children serve God faithfully all their lives. Somewhere along the way, though, many parents forget that our children belong to Him. The fact is, mom and dad are not the ultimate authority over children's career paths, or what goals they will seek and actually achieve. God is the authority. He holds the plan, and we must release our kids to His purposes.

Second, Hannah's promise reminds us to keep the promises we make in prayer. The old saying, "Danger past, God forgotten," is often true. We make promises to God in prayer that we do not keep once our crisis is over. We have seen people on hospital beds who have promised, "I know God is going to make me well, and I'm going to serve Jesus from now on." Then healing comes, and they go back to living their lives just as before. The sincerity of Hannah's prayer is seen by the fact that she not only made a promise to God but kept her word.

IN TUNE OR OUT OF TUNE?

Eli was the high priest at Shiloh. He was sitting by the door of the tabernacle when Hannah came into the tabernacle. Watching. He saw her lips moving without speaking. Thinking Hannah was drunk from the sacrificial meal, Eli said, "How long will you be drunk? Put your wine away from you!" (1 Sam. 1:14).

Hannah's heart was full of affection for God, and Eli accused her of being a drunk. He should have known better. While some people become tearful when they are inebriated, they would not have the attitude of prayer of Hannah. Nor was Hannah loud and boisterous like most drunken worshippers would have been. Eli was so caught up in the evil of his day that he didn't recognize a genuinely broken, contrite spirit when he saw one.

Why would the priest interrupt someone as she was crying out to the Lord? Didn't he discern her devotion to God? Eli's own family was heading toward destruction, and perhaps Eli's heart was so out of fellowship with God that he was blind to brokenhearted prayer.

His sons, Hophni and Phinehas, served with him in offering sacrifices. These two corrupt and wicked men sinned against the Lord by taking the best offerings for themselves and by sleeping with women at the very door of the tabernacle. Eli had chosen to honor his sons above God. He refused to deal decisively with their sin. As a result, Eli's heart had grown cold toward God. He was so far away from God that he couldn't see the love and devotion Hannah had for the Lord.

Hannah could have responded to Eli's charges. If Eli's sons had begun their misuse of the tabernacle at this time, she could have put Eli in his place by reminding him of their wickedness. She could have gotten angry that Eli would treat a worshipper so rudely. Instead, she showed respect: "No, my lord, I am a woman of sorrowful spirit. I have drunk neither wine nor intoxicating drink, but have poured out my soul before the LORD. Do not consider your maidservant a wicked woman, for out of the abundance of my complaint and grief I have spoken until now" (1 Sam. 1:15–16).

Hannah was humble toward Eli. She didn't want him to consider her a wicked woman. She honored his authority by calling herself his maidservant. Moved by Hannah's explanation, Eli performed his priestly duty. He blessed Hannah and sent her on her way, saying, "Go in peace, and the God of Israel grant your petition which you have asked of Him" (1 Sam. 1:17).

Their responses show the difference between a life that is in tune with God and one that is out of tune. Because Hannah's life was in tune with God, she was humble and compassionate—even when mistreated. Eli was quick to judge and harsh because his life was out of tune with the Lord.

When we are faithful in prayer, God will keep our lives in tune with Him. We will be able to see the best in others and act compassionately toward them because we see them through the eyes of the Lord.

Is your life in tune with God or out of tune? If you are spending time with God in prayer and Bible study, it will be evident in the smile on your face and the words from your mouth. Does your mouth praise God? Does your life shine with the light of Jesus? "For you were once darkness, but now you are light in the Lord. Walk as children of light" (Eph. 5:8). "Let your light so shine before men, that they may see your good works and glorify your Father in heaven" (Matt. 5:16).

AN UNLIKELY PEACE

Hannah's story begins with turmoil, but it ends with great joy. Hearing Eli's blessing, she responded, "Let your maidservant find favor in your sight." Then, she "went her way and ate, and her face was no longer sad" (1 Sam. 1:18).

When we come to the Lord in heartbroken prayer, we will leave His presence changed forever. God gives us the hope and strength to live the Christian life day by day. "Be anxious for nothing, but in everything by prayer and supplication, with thanksgiving, let your requests be made known to God; and the peace of God, which surpasses all understanding, will guard your hearts and minds through Christ Jesus" (Phil. 4:6–7). When we pray to the Lord, He energizes our lives to live for Him. He gives us a peace that no one can understand.

The air was chilly on that February morning as Stephen and I walked with our son, Joshua, toward my obstetrician's office.

"Will we really get to see the baby?" asked Joshua excitedly. He was five years old and thrilled at the prospect of being a big brother.

"Yes, we will, buddy," Stephen answered. "You're going to get your first look at your little brother or sister."

In a few minutes, we were all watching as the doctor began the ultrasound. Almost as soon as the procedure began, the expression on the doctor's face told me something wasn't right.

"I'm not seeing any growth from last time," he said. "And I'm not detecting a heartbeat."

The doctor continued to examine the unmoving image on the screen. "I'm so sorry," he said.

In shocked grief, we found ourselves sitting down with Joshua to explain that his baby brother or sister had died. We all cried. The next day, at eleven weeks of pregnancy, I was admitted to the hospital, where Stephen and I wept again as I miscarried.

During those two tragic days, and in the times of grief that followed, both Stephen and I experienced what can best be described as an unlikely peace. God replaced the sorrow with a sense of calmness and stillness beyond our ability to explain or describe. We knew God had a plan for our lives, and that brought peace.

When we go through heartaches, God gives us peace. He sustains and guides us. As we turn our heartaches over to the Lord, His peace will give us a joy that only comes through knowing Him.

SUGGESTED SCRIPTURE READING

Psalm 27

PRAYER GUIDE

Ask God to reveal to your heart that . . .

- God is your light and salvation.
- you can seek God and dwell in His presence.
- God is your Rock in times of trouble.
- it is good to sing praises to the Lord, even in times of trouble.
- God will never leave or forsake you.
- the Lord will take care of you.
- you can seek God's direction.
- you can wait on the Lord.

Day 11

TRUSTING GOD'S TIMING

For this child I prayed, and the
LORD has granted me my petition
which I asked of Him. Therefore
I also have lent him to the LORD.
(1 Sam. 1:27–28a)

Prayer delights God's ear, it melts
His heart, it opens His hand: God
cannot deny a praying soul.
　　　　　　　　—Thomas Watson[1]

*G*od remembers your prayers.

"Now, don't forget this note," I said. "It's very important that you take it with you today. I'm going to put it in your front shirt pocket so that you will remember to take it out. I've written the name of the person you need to give it to on the front of the envelope."

With that, I gave him a kiss and sent him on his way—not my little boy but my husband. I have learned how much Stephen relies on me to help him remember things.

What do you do when you want to make sure you remember something? You might write an appointment on your calendar or program a date into your "personal digital assistant." You might put a "sticky note" on your kitchen countertop or even tie a string around your finger (Have you ever actually known someone to tie a string around his or her finger?).

HE NEVER FORGETS

Maybe you have prayed and wondered whether God remembers. You might begin to ask, "Has He written my request down somewhere? Is the answer on His schedule for the future? Does He have a string tied around *His* finger?"

Hannah discovered the precious truth that our God never forgets our prayers. Grief stricken yet trusting, she had asked God to give her a son. She had promised that she would devote that child to the Lord. Comforted by the blessing Eli the priest had spoken over her, she left the tabernacle. Now, her time of waiting had begun. In the weeks and months ahead, Hannah remembered the Lord and the Lord remembered her.

REMEMBERING TO WORSHIP

After the annual feast and ceremonies at Shiloh, Hannah's husband, Elkanah, and the rest of the family got up early to return home to Ramah. Before they began their long journey, however, they worshipped the Lord as a family. "Then they rose early in the morning and worshiped before the LORD" (1 Sam. 1:19a).

We can imagine that Elkanah observed something different about Hannah that morning. Her praise to the Lord seemed to have awakened. She was worshipping with joy, as in earlier years. Peninnah also may have noticed a difference in Hannah. No longer was her rival's head bowed in sorrow. Knowing that the Lord had heard her prayer, Hannah must have taken new delight in worshipping God.

Strengthened prayer begins with strong worship. We can worship God in a variety of times and places. We worship God privately. We worship God in the fellowship of other believers. We worship

God in our families in times of devotional Bible reading, prayer, and singing. Family worship time might be in the morning around the breakfast table, when you read God's Word and pray as a family. Or you may choose to do family devotions after the evening meal or at some other time. Our family spends time together in prayer, Bible study, and worship each evening in our son's room.

Stephen and I started a family prayer time together as newlyweds. Each day, we have tried to take time to pray and read the Bible as a couple. Though there have been times when we have been incredibly busy with school, church, and career, our goal has been to honor the Lord in this way in our marriage.

The arrival of our son Joshua added an exciting new dynamic to our family worship. We began including him in our devotions from the day he came home from the hospital. Long before he was old enough to understand what we were doing, we read Scripture, prayed, and sang songs of worship to the Lord with Joshua.

Making worship a priority in your home teaches everyone in the family to lean on your heavenly Father. Families that read God's Word, pray, and sing praises to God realize that God is in control.

While waiting on God to answer prayer, you can live a life of worship by . . .

- *participating with the church in worship.* Sometimes we attend church without worshipping. We may spend public worship time enjoying or critiquing the "performance" of the preacher, the singers, or other participants. We miss the opportunity to meet God with our fellow members in the body of Christ.
- *taking time for personal worship.* As part of our private prayer and Bible study time each day, we can come before God in worship. We may sing hymns or other songs of praise or we may simply spend a few moments meditating on Him and what we read in His Word. We need personal time in God's presence each day.
- *leading in family worship.* As noted above, every home needs a time for family worship, just as we need time together in

other activities. Especially if there are children, whether very young or teenagers, dads and moms can lead in a brief family devotional time each day. God blesses times of family worship, drawing families closer to Him and one another.

REMEMBERING HANNAH'S PRAYER

Almost as soon as Elkanah's family returned home, God answered Hannah's prayer. "And Elkanah knew Hannah his wife, and the LORD remembered her" (1 Sam. 1:19b). The Hebrew word translated "remember" often refers to a response that occurs after something is called to mind. In response to Hannah's prayer, the Lord remembered her request. Out of mercy and love, He opened Hannah's womb.

"So it came to pass in the process of time that Hannah conceived and bore a son, and called his name Samuel, saying, 'Because I have asked for him from the LORD'" (1 Sam. 1:20). In Hebrew, Samuel's name sounds similar to "heard by God." Hannah asked God for him, and God honored Hannah, His humble servant, by allowing her to give birth to a son.

God wants us to wait patiently on Him in prayer as Hannah did. Likely she had prayed many years for a child. God upheld Hannah during all that time. He answered her prayer when His timing was right and her heart was right. Then came the *yes*.

God always answers our prayers, but not always with the positive response given to Hannah.

Sometimes He says *yes* and sends His answer immediately. On those occasions, we can praise God for His provision and act in thankfulness for what we have received from His hand.

Other times, God will answer *no*. He may not even make clear why He answered that way. He doesn't have to explain Himself. We can simply trust that *no* was the best answer, praise God for His love, and continue to seek His will.

Often, God will answer, **wait**. God may ask us to wait for any of a number of reasons. The timing might not be right. We may not be ready for the answer, though we believe we are. God may want to refine our request. That could have been what He did in Hannah's life. Perhaps when she started praying for a child, she was not yet ready for complete surrender of the child to Him. After making her ready, He miraculously provided.

As we wait on God, we can trust that He is working to tune our desires to His. "Now this is the confidence that we have in Him, that if we ask anything according to His will, He hears us" (1 John 5:14). God knows the very best things for us, so He directs our hearts to His will.

REMEMBERING OUR PROMISES

The time came for Elkanah and his family to travel again to Shiloh for the yearly sacrifice. Hannah talked with her husband about staying behind to take care of baby Samuel. Since the baby was very young and still nursing, Elkanah agreed with Hannah that she should stay home with Samuel. He told her, "Do what seems best to you; wait until you have weaned him. Only let the LORD establish His word" (1 Sam. 1:23b).

Elkanah and Hannah wanted to keep the vow they had made to the Lord. Their hearts desired to be true to God. When Hannah was finished nursing, she kept her vow by giving Samuel to the Lord. "Now when she had weaned him, she took him up with her . . . and brought him to the house of the LORD in Shiloh. And the child was young" (1 Sam. 1:24). At the right time, Hannah gave Samuel to God, just as she had promised.

When you make a promise to God, do you keep it? We are quick to make promises in times of difficulty:

- "God, I'm going to read Your Word and pray every day."
- "God, I'm going to become faithful in my giving."
- "God, I'm going to become more involved in serving You at my church."
- "God, I'm going to lay aside this sinful habit and start living for You."

Sometimes such promises are attempts to bargain with God. When the stress is over, the promises we made vanish from our memories. Failing to keep our promises to God is serious business. God says, "When you make a vow to the LORD your God, you shall not delay to pay it; for the LORD your God will surely require it of you, and it would be sin to you" (Deut. 23:21). The psalmist wrote, "Vows made to You are binding upon me, O God" (Ps. 56:12a). We sin when we promise something to God, then break our word. But that's not what Hannah did. When she promised to give her newborn son to God, she meant it, and she kept her promise. Hannah was honoring God by giving the child Samuel back to the Lord. God is faithful and true to every promise He makes. The Bible declares, "You are God, and Your words are true" (2 Sam. 7:28a). We can reflect His character by keeping our word to our heavenly Father.

REMEMBERING TO PRAISE GOD

Hannah brought God an offering of a bull, flour, and wine to seal her vow to the Lord (1 Sam. 1:24), but her ultimate sacrifice was bringing Samuel to Eli the priest. She said to Eli, "O my lord! As your soul lives, my lord, I am the woman who stood by you here, praying to the LORD. For this child I prayed, and the LORD has granted me my petition which I asked of Him. Therefore I also have lent him to the LORD; as long as he lives he shall be lent to the LORD" (1 Sam. 1:26–28a).

Eli didn't know what Hannah had prayed to the Lord that day in the tabernacle. Now she had the opportunity to tell him and to praise God for His answer. Hannah gave God praise for answering her prayer. Now Eli knew the blessing God had given to Elkanah and Hannah.

First Samuel 1:27–28 demonstrates her attitude about her young son: "The LORD has granted me my petition which I asked of Him. Therefore I also have lent him to the LORD." In the Hebrew language, the word translated "lent" can be translated "granted." Hannah was saying, "God gave this child to me, so I'm giving this child to God."

She gave her son back to the Lord so that Samuel was set apart to serve God faithfully all of his life. Samuel—God's blessing to Hannah—would grow up to become a blessing to all Israel.

Hannah revealed a heartbeat of praise. When we understand that everything we have comes from God, we are openhanded in giving to Him praise and thanksgiving.

We give praise to God by giving our time and abilities to Him. God has gifted every believer to serve Him and to be a blessing to others. He has given us life and breath so that we can use our time to honor Him. We belong to Him, not to ourselves. Our talents and our time are His.

We give praise to God by giving our children to Him. As parents, we have been entrusted with a great honor from God. He has given us little ones to train up to love and serve the Lord. While bringing children to church to worship and study God's Word is vital to their spiritual growth, the greatest responsibility to train our children in God's Word, prayer, and worship belongs to parents. Our highest goal as parents should be to lead our children into a growing relationship with Jesus Christ, and then to release them to God to become whatever He wants them to be.

We give praise to God by giving our resources to Him. God has commanded that we give Him the tithe and our offerings (Mal. 3:8–10) out of praise and thanksgiving for what He has given us. Even more, He wants us to say, "God, my home, my car, my possessions, and everything with which You have blessed me belong to You. I dedicate them all to You and Your glory."

ON HOLD

You call to order a pizza, the restaurant answers, and before you have time to speak, the voice on the other end of the line says, "Can you hold?" Or, you call your insurance company to ask an important question about your policy, and the cheerful voice on an automated message says, "All lines are busy. Please hold, and the first available associate will be glad to help you." Music begins to play, and every now and then a taped voice assures you that your call will be answered. You wait and wait with the phone to your ear. You may even start humming some of the songs that are playing. After a while, you begin to wonder if you've been forgotten.

Sometimes we feel like God has put our prayer on hold. We have been praying about something urgent, and nothing happens. We ask, "Has God forgotten me?"

We have His assurance that He has not forgotten. During the time we seem to be on hold, God is making us ready for the answer. He remembers, and He wants us to remember Him.

SUGGESTED SCRIPTURE READING

Deuteronomy 6:1–9

PRAYER GUIDE

Seek God in prayer by . . .

- praising God for His Word.
- asking for a heart of obedience to His Word.
- praising God for being the one true God.
- asking God to give you His love so you can love Him wholeheartedly.
- praising God for giving you the ability to read, learn, and memorize His Word.
- asking God to guide you in teaching His Word to your children.
- meditating on Deuteronomy 6:5: "You shall love the LORD your God with all your heart, with all your soul, and with all your strength."

Day 12

Praising Our God

And Hannah prayed and said:

"My heart rejoices in the LORD;
My horn is exalted in the LORD."
(1 Sam. 2:1a)

Praise is our rent, our tribute. We
are unjust if we do not pay it.
—Matthew Henry[1]

Praise adorns genuine prayer.

Sara, a green-eyed girl in the seventh grade with freckles and rusty brown hair, had picked out a Mother's Day card for her mom. She was proud of her independence this year. Her older sister hadn't had to remind her to get it. She had even managed to buy the card on the sly while she and her dad were out shopping.

The card was really important to Sara this year.

The previous summer, Sara had been diagnosed with a large tumor in her abdomen. She had cried in her mom's arms when the doctor said it might be cancer. Although the biopsy had revealed no cancer, Sara's surgery and lengthy recovery had been hard for everyone. Her mom had been by her side all the way—cheering Sara up when she was stuck in bed, helping her keep up with her school assignments, and praying with her each day.

This Mother's Day seemed the right time to let her mom know how much her love had meant. She wrote a message inside the card, sealed the envelope, and put "Mom" on the front. But that didn't seem to be enough. She wanted to do something more. Sara went into the drawer of her desk, pulled out glitter, multicolored markers, and glue, and began to decorate the envelope. Soon, she had covered it with hearts, stars, swirls, and sparkles. Now she was ready to give her mom the card. It really was beautiful.

Our prayers become more beautiful in God's sight when they are covered with praise. As we praise God and thank Him for what He has done, He is pleased with our prayers. While the Bible overflows with praise to God, no song of praise in Scripture is more beautiful than Hannah's, recorded in 1 Samuel 2:1–10. After Hannah gave Samuel to the Lord, she offered to God her praise.

Hannah's prayer of praise is mirrored in the song of Mary after she had conceived the Lord Jesus (Luke 1:46–55). Both Hannah and Mary magnified the Lord. They praised God for His holiness and strength. The two women exalted God for giving to them their special children. Many Bible scholars believe that Mary knew Hannah's prayer and used it as a model for her own.

REJOICING IN THE LORD

Hannah brought Samuel to the tabernacle when he was around three years old. Just as she had promised, she devoted her firstborn son fully to the Lord. Hannah brought Samuel to the temple in Shiloh to leave him there with Eli the priest. Though Samuel was very young, he would serve in the Lord's house, assisting Eli.

We cannot help but think that Hannah felt sorrow as she prepared to leave her little boy with the priest at Shiloh. Her home was far away. She would not be there to watch Samuel each day. Hannah could have thrown a pity party for herself as she gave her son to God. Instead, Hannah focused on the Lord and rejoiced in Him, praying, "My heart rejoices in the LORD; my horn is exalted in the LORD. I smile at my enemies, because I rejoice in Your salvation" (1 Sam. 2:1–2).

Notice the words Hannah said. Hannah's love and devotion to God overflowed from her heart. Though her circumstances were bittersweet, her heart was happy because of the Lord. Had she placed her joy in Samuel, she might have been unable to rejoice that day. But instead, Hannah's focus was on the Lord. She was rejoicing in the God who gave her Samuel. The Lord was the delight of Hannah's heart.

Sometimes we make the mistake of rejoicing in our circumstances rather than in our Lord. If we rejoice in our health, or in our prosperity, or even in our family, then our praise will ebb and flow like the capricious tides. Our joy will fade should our health fail, or our prosperity wither, or our family suffer crisis. If we rejoice in our God, however, our reason for rejoicing will never go away, because His love and mercy endure forever.

Hannah then exclaimed, "My horn is exalted." The horn was a symbol of strength. Hannah praised God because He had strengthened her and given Samuel to her. She had been very weak, but God had exalted her horn, increasing her strength.

Next, Hannah prayed, "I smile at my enemies, because I rejoice in Your salvation." Literally, her words are: "My mouth is enlarged at my enemies." Undoubtedly, her enemies included Peninnah, who had insulted Hannah for years because she was unable to have children. Her enemies might have included others who mocked Hannah's barrenness. If a Hebrew woman was unable to have children, she was looked down upon for her infertility. Her enemies caused her suffering and shame.

We can picture Hannah's facial expression as she endured ridicule because she was childless. Her mouth had been drawn. Her lips may have quivered as she tried to hold back her tears. Now, Hannah no longer had to be silent or sad. She could greet Peninnah with a happy face and a song of praise. Hannah smiled at her enemies because God answered her prayer and gave her a son. God's deliverance had brought a joy to her heart that shone on her face. God had turned her sorrow into overwhelming joy.

Do you start your prayer time in thanksgiving and praise to God? Every day, we have numerous things to thank God for. Just think of the things for which you can give God praise:

- Praise God for being able to awake from a night of sleep.
- Praise God for being who He says He is.
- Praise God for forgiveness.
- Praise God for His creative power.
- Praise God for His daily provision.
- Praise God for His will for your life.
- Praise God for life's encouragements.
- Praise God for rain, snow, and sunshine, and the beauty of the world He has made.
- Praise God for the courage to face challenges.
- Praise God for the problems that help you grow stronger.
- Praise God for the special talents and gifts He has given you.
- Praise God for your country.
- Praise God for your family.
- Praise God that He gave the Holy Spirit to live within you.
- Praise God that He gave the Bible, His precious Word, to His people.
- Praise God that He knows you better than you know yourself.
- Praise God that Jesus Christ died for your sins.

HOLY IS THE LORD

Hannah began to praise God for His holiness. She cried out, "No one is holy like the LORD, for there is none besides You, nor is there any rock like our God" (1 Sam. 2:2). Hannah's praise is a testimony that the Lord God stands alone. He alone is holy. He alone is a rock of faithfulness. He alone is God.

"There is none besides You." Hannah proclaimed that no god compares to the true and living God of Israel. Hannah realized there is only one true God. God's power was unrivaled then, and He continues to be without equal today. Many people today may think that all paths lead to God or that one faith is just as valid as another. Believers in Christ understand, however, that we worship and have an eternal relationship with the one true God who controls everything.

"Nor is there any rock like our God." Hannah knew that her God was like a rock. Just as rock is solid and immovable, God's strength gave her stability and refuge. God provided strength for Hannah to stand. She realized God was unchangeable and trustworthy. God was the rock on which Hannah placed her faith. He alone could handle Hannah's burdens.

Because of our unholiness, we have a hard time relating to the holiness of God. When we pray, we are coming into the holy presence of God. Once we really start to praise the Lord for His holiness, we'll begin to live our lives in holy reverence to Him.

Rich and his wife, Sandra, rented a small apartment while they were finishing college. After a few months, Sandra made an announcement: "Rich, I think we should paint this living room. The walls are so dingy. Just a coat of paint would make a big difference."

The next day Rich contacted the building superintendent and got permission to paint. He bought a gallon of white paint that afternoon. He and Sandra began the project early Saturday morning. They draped drop cloths on the carpet and all their furniture. As Rich was taping newspaper over the thermostat control, he remarked, "This thermostat cover is the only thing white on this wall."

Sandra agreed. The white plastic cover did stand out against the dirty walls.

They finished painting by noon, went out for lunch and shopped to give the walls time to dry. Then they returned home and began to uncover their furniture and put things back into place.

"Would you look at that," Rich said, chuckling.

He had taken the paper off the thermostat control. The plastic cover that had looked so white and clean that morning now looked dirty and dingy. What had happened? The thermostat cover had been dirty that morning, but now, against the freshly painted white wall, its uncleanness showed.

In the same way, we can fool ourselves into thinking that we are pure and righteous, but when we are confronted with the holiness of our God, we begin to see just how unclean we are. God is the holy Lord. He alone is perfect and without blemish. He alone is pure and blameless. He alone is sinless. God is holy, holy, holy!

As we praise God daily for His holiness, He will show us how we can become more holy. Greater still, He will work within us to make us more like Himself.

THE GOD OF KNOWLEDGE

Next, Hannah started to praise God for His knowledge. She prayed: "Talk no more so very proudly; let no arrogance come from your mouth, for the LORD is the God of knowledge; and by Him actions are weighed" (1 Sam. 2:3).

To whom was Hannah speaking when she said, "Talk no more so very proudly"? Maybe she was thinking about boasts of Peninnah, who had used her children to denigrate Hannah. Or, she may have been reminding herself not to be arrogant now that God had chosen to bless her with a child. Especially as Samuel grew and became a great leader in Israel, Hannah would need to guard against pride over her son. Whatever else she meant, she was offering a word of exhortation to everyone who heard her, including us.

Hannah admonished all who would brag about themselves. We all have moments of pride and arrogance. We brag on our children. We boast about our job. We arrogantly talk about possessions.

When pride creeps in, we're in a spiritual danger zone. "Pride goes before destruction, and a haughty spirit before a fall. Better to be of a humble spirit with the lowly, than to divide the spoil with the proud" (Prov. 16:18–19). Pride and arrogance leave us unable to praise holy God, because He opposes the proud (James 4:6). That's why Hannah cautioned others—and maybe even herself—to hold pride and arrogance in check.

Pride dwells excessively on our own needs. It may be that we are not praising God in our prayer time because we are overly concerned with telling God about our problems. As she praised God, Hannah kept her focus on the Lord. "For the LORD is the God of knowledge," she prayed, "and by Him actions are weighed" (1 Sam. 2:3b). Hannah praised God for His knowledge.

Hannah realized that God knows all. She praised God for knowing the right actions to take with her and others. God knew how to provide for Israel in battle. God knew how to deal with Israel when the people sinned. God knew how to help Hannah in her needs. Hannah thanked God for knowing the right way to deal with her situation.

God's knowledge and judgment are always right. He knows how to reward us. He knows how to convict us of sin. God knows how to lift us up. He knows how to penetrate our sin-stained hearts. He knows how to guide our steps when we call on Him.

A FINAL SONG OF PRAISE

An elderly Christian man, who had always been a fine singer, learned that he had cancer of the tongue. He would have to have surgery to stop the cancer from spreading.

After everything was ready for his operation, the man looked up at his doctor and asked, "Are you sure I will never sing again?"

The surgeon found it difficult to answer his question. He simply nodded his head. The old man then asked if he could sit up for a moment.

"I've had many good times singing the praises of God," he said. "And now you tell me I can never sing again. I have one song that will be my last. It will be of gratitude and praise to God."

With his doctor by his side, the man began to sing softly but confidently the words of an Isaac Watts hymn:

I'll praise my Maker while I've Breath,
And when my voice is lost in death,
Praise shall employ my nobler power;
My days of praise shall ne'er be past,
While life, and thought, and being last,
Or immortality endures.
                    (Isaac Watts, "Psalm 146," 1714)

God desires our praise. Hannah's song helps us realize the importance of praising Him. We can begin to praise holy God in prayer today. While our lips and tongues can form the words and while our minds can compose the thoughts, let's find time in prayer to praise our God.

SUGGESTED SCRIPTURE READING

Psalm 113

PRAYER GUIDE

God can use His Word to empower our prayer lives. Use Psalm 113 as a prayer.

- Quote back each verse to the Lord as a prayer of praise.
- Add your own praises to those you find in this psalm.

Day 13

RECOGNIZING GOD'S SOVEREIGNTY

For the pillars of the earth are the
LORD's, and He has set the world
upon them. (1 Sam. 2:8c)

There is no attribute more com-
forting to His children than that of
God's sovereignty. Under the most
adverse circumstances, in the most
severe trials, they believe that sovereignty has ordained their afflic-
tions, that sovereignty overrules
them, and that sovereignty will
sanctify them all.
—C. H. Spurgeon[1]

Prayer acknowledges God's sovereignty.

Who's in charge? That question may be the most important issue
we ever have to settle in our spiritual lives.

Susan, the young mother of a three-year-old son, had been struggling with him all morning. First, Thomas didn't want to get out of bed. Then, he didn't want to get dressed. Then, he fussed over his breakfast cereal. Exasperated, she looked him in the eye and asked the question that she was certain would bring him into line: "Thomas, who is in charge here?"

Without missing a beat, the Sunday school born and bred toddler replied, "Jesus is!"[2]

That's having the right answer at the wrong time.

Still, it *is* the right answer: Jesus is in charge here. In our homes, in our churches, in our careers, and in every other aspect of who we are, the Lord God alone has the right to be in charge. He has the right to do as He wishes with His creation. God reigns over everything and everyone.

One of the things God does in our prayer lives is to show us how He reigns over the circumstances of our lives. We experience God's sovereignty through prayer.

The second part of Hannah's prayer of praise emphasizes God's sovereignty. Like many of the poems in the book of Psalms, Hannah's song of praise uses poetic contrasts to describe God's dominion over human circumstances. She calls attention to God's sovereignty in His power and in His protection.

SOVEREIGN IN HIS POWER

In 1 Samuel 2:4–8, Hannah speaks of several ways that God demonstrates His sovereign power. Because God reigns in His power, He has the ability to do anything. God says that nothing is too difficult for Him (Jer. 32:27).

First, God has the power to bring victory. "The bows of the mighty men are broken," Hannah prayed, "and those who stumbled are girded with strength" (1 Sam. 2:4). Hannah pictures the bows of mighty archers being snapped like twigs by God's power, while the Lord fills His ragtag army with strength.

Hannah experienced God's power to bring triumph to her life.

When she felt defeated by her inability to bear a child, God proved Himself strong. He accomplished the impossible in her life.

Hannah knew that the same power that had brought her personal victory could bring military victory to her weak nation. Throughout the Old Testament, Israel prospered and defeated enemies when they followed God. When Israel failed to trust in God, He allowed their enemies to defeat them. God has supreme control. King David proclaimed, "Some trust in chariots, and some in horses; but we will remember the name of the LORD our God" (Ps. 20:7).

It is foolish for us to lean on our arms of flesh when we can be upheld by God's power. When Hannah prayed for God to give her a son, she was asking for Him to do something she was powerless to do. By His own sovereignty, God proved Himself strong in her life. In the same way, God wants believers to rely on His power completely. Too often, we try to take the reins of our lives and make something happen, when our only victory is found in trusting in His strength.

God also has the power to supply our needs. In 1 Samuel 2:5, Hannah presents another set of contrasts: "Those who were full have hired themselves out for bread, and the hungry have ceased to hunger. Even the barren has borne seven, and she who has many children has become feeble." Not only does God have the power to bring victory or defeat to an army, He also possesses the ability to feed the hungry and cause those who have much to become poor. Greater still, Hannah proclaimed, the Lord has the supreme power to cause a woman to have children and to make another woman cease having children. Hannah understood that her welfare depended completely on God's power.

Lois needed $153.27 by 2 PM, and it was 1:30. She sat in her car outside a restaurant where she had just eaten lunch with a group of women from her church. When it had come time to pay for the meal, she had used her last $20, picking up the tab for a guest missionary from Romania.

As a result of cancer surgery, Lois suffered from lymphedema, a condition that caused tremendous swelling in her arm. God had healed the cancer, but the swelling remained. Lois had been invited to attend a workshop on the disease in Indianapolis. Ordinarily, the seminar was open only to healthcare professionals. Knowing the great interest Lois had in the subject, her physical therapist had arranged for her to attend. Every expense would be paid—except for the plane fare of $153.27.

Lois eagerly accepted the invitation, and then started asking God to help provide money for her to go. Her family's budget was stretched tight because of the medical bills she had incurred during the cancer treatments. But Lois believed God had provided this opportunity to learn about new treatments that could alleviate her pain. She was to meet her friend in a half hour at the travel agency to pick up the plane ticket. She still didn't have the money.

"God will provide for my need," she said to herself as she clutched her keys in her hand and laid back against the headrest. Her certainty, however, had begun to waver.

Just then, Lois glanced in her rearview mirror and saw a small black sports car back out, then pull back into its parking space. She recognized the driver as Beverly Easton from her luncheon group. Lois wondered if Beverly was having car trouble when Beverly slowly drove out of the parking lot, circled the restaurant, and pulled back in again. Beverly stopped in the middle of the lot, got out, walked toward Lois's car, and stuck her head through Lois's open passenger window.

"I know you don't know me very well, and I hope you don't think I'm crazy," Beverly said. "I'm so embarrassed. Please don't be offended by this."

Lois's curiosity was stirred. "What's the matter, Beverly?"

"Well," she hesitated. "Several months ago God told me to put change in an envelope for you. I've just carried it around. I've added to it every day until I got the nerve to give it to you. I hope this isn't insulting."

Her face flamed red as she tossed a bulging envelope onto the car seat.

"I just have to obey God," Beverly mumbled, darting to her car before Lois could respond.

Makeup smudges and ink smears covered the once white envelope. On the front, Lois's name was scribbled in big letters. With
tears in her eyes, she carefully emptied the contents out on the seat
and started counting. There were bills of all denominations and lots
of change. The envelope contained exactly $153.27.[3]

God has the ability to provide for our needs. Sometimes He does it
through dramatic and unusual means—as when He provided those
funds for Lois. He may even provide by miraculous intervention—as
when He gave a baby to Hannah. More often, though, God provides
for us in commonplace ways. We must never forget to see His hand
in the everyday provision He brings into our lives. When our lives
are centered on prayer, we become increasingly aware of His care
and provision—and increasingly thankful.

God has the power to give life. Hannah realized God's sovereignty
over life and death. "The LORD kills and makes alive; He brings
down to the grave and brings up" (1 Sam. 2:6). Hannah praised God
for His power over life and death. She saw how God had brought life
into her family through Samuel. Hannah proclaimed God's control
over all life.

We can praise God for giving us physical life. "For You formed my
inward parts," the psalmist says; "You covered me in my mother's
womb. I will praise You, for I am fearfully and wonderfully made"
(Ps. 139:13–14a). We can also praise Him for making eternal life
available to us through faith in Christ. Paul wrote, "I have been crucified with Christ; it is no longer I who live, but Christ lives in me;
and the life which I now live in the flesh I live by faith in the Son of
God, who loved me and gave Himself for me" (Gal. 2:20).

Through His sovereign power, God controls the length of each life
and made the way for us to spend eternity with Him. Our lives are
truly in His hands.

SOVEREIGN IN HIS PROTECTION

In response to God's sovereignty, Hannah also praised God for
sustaining the world and protecting His people. With a joyful voice,

she sang, "For the pillars of the earth are the LORD's, and He has set the world upon them. He will guard the feet of His saints, but the wicked shall be silent in darkness. For by strength no man shall prevail" (1 Sam. 2:8c–9).

God's supreme power is revealed in His creation. God established the pillars, or foundations, of the earth. Not only does He sustain the earth, but He protects those who walk in His paths. "He will guard the feet of His saints." As God's people kept His commandments and obeyed Him, God would keep their feet from slipping. God would keep their lives on the right path as they followed Him. Meanwhile, those who rejected God found themselves "in darkness," separated from His love, His light, and His life.

Hannah praised God for His protection that came down from heaven. "The adversaries of the LORD shall be broken in pieces; from heaven He will thunder against them. The LORD will judge the ends of the earth" (1 Sam. 2:10). She understood that those who oppose the Lord would not win. He would judge the wicked for their rebellion against Him and their hostility toward His children.

Hannah praised God's protection of His people and contrasted the security of the saints with the doom of those who refuse to follow God. Those that rejected God would face darkness and hell. Hannah realized that holy God would protect and guide her as she followed Him, and that God would judge those who turned from Him. God's sovereignty will neither allow His people to perish nor sin to go unpunished.

A SOVEREIGN SAVIOR

Hannah ended her prayer of praise by pointing to King Jesus. "He will give strength to His king, and exalt the horn of His anointed" (1 Sam. 2:10c). Hannah's prayer marks the first time in Scripture that the Lord's Anointed is mentioned. Hannah realized God was going to send a Messiah—someone to save the people of Israel from their enemies and from their sins. God would need to send a ruler to be King of Kings. God would exalt Him higher than the kings of the earth (Ps. 89:27).

Hannah expected Israel's coming king, whether or not she knew that the king would be anointed by her son. She knew that in His sovereignty, God had provided for the future, and someday God would send the true Anointed One, with all strength and power. Hannah praised God for His protection for her and Israel at that moment and in the future.

Though Hannah had only a cloudy and incomplete understanding of all that Jesus Christ would be and the extent of what He would do, she gave Him praise. Are you praising God for King Jesus? Are you excited about spending eternity with the King of kings? As we cry out to our sovereign God for all of His blessings, we can praise Him for Jesus in particular.

Hannah's devotion to the Lord brought God's blessing on her life. God provided for Hannah by giving her three more sons and two daughters (1 Sam. 2:21). Hannah's first son, Samuel, grew up and ministered before the Lord (1 Sam. 2:18, 21). Hannah honored God with her life, and God honored Hannah.

Hannah discovered the source of the believer's praise. Our praise does not flow from the prayers God answers, no matter how deeply felt those prayers may be. Our praise does not flow from the gifts God gives, no matter how wonderful these gifts are. The true source of the believer's praise is the giver, our sovereign Lord.

CUTS AND BLOWS

In 1905, diamond mine superintendent Frederick Wells came upon a magnificent diamond in a South African mine. The Cullinan diamond remains the largest gem diamond ever discovered. The stone eventually was presented as a gift to Edward VII of England by the Transvaal government. The king sent the three thousand-carat diamond to Amsterdam to be cut. There, it was put into the hands of an expert gem cutter.

The cutter studied the stone for months, then cut a notch in it. Then he broke the beautiful jewel into pieces.

Did he do this out of recklessness, wastefulness, or carelessness? No. He made drawings and models of the gem in preparation for breaking it. He studied its quality, its defects, and its lines of cleavage. When he struck the blow that broke the diamond, he did the one thing that would bring that gem to its most perfect shapeliness, radiance, and splendor. The blow that seemed to ruin the precious stone was, in fact, its perfect redemption. From the broken stone, he crafted nine magnificent gems and numerous smaller stones that his skilled eye had seen hidden in the uncut stone.[4]

Sometimes, God allows a stinging blow to fall. He allowed that to happen to Hannah. For years, she wondered why she was left childless. For years, she endured the taunts of her rival. God's people suffer at times, and our souls cry out in agony. The pain may take the form of a wayward child, or a chronic illness, or a stalled career, or something else that dims our hopes.

The cuts and blows God allows may seem to be terrible mistakes. We wonder, "Why is God letting this happen?" But it is no mistake. You are the most priceless jewel in the world to God. And He is the most skillful gem cutter in the universe. In His sovereignty, He knows just how to deal with us.

SUGGESTED SCRIPTURE READING

Psalm 34:1–8

PRAYER GUIDE

Rejoice in the Lord by . . .

- magnifying God with a song.
- praising God for hearing your prayers.
- thanking God for His salvation.
- praising God for His deliverance.
- thanking God for being your Lord.
- looking out your window and praising God for all you see.

Day 14

Bringing Your Needs to God

*W*e have seen the way God answered Hannah's prayers—giving her a son miraculously and exalting her soul from overwhelming sorrow to inexpressible joy.

We've only seen the beginning of this story, though. The book of 1 Samuel goes on to tell the mighty way that God used Hannah's son to stand for Him in Israel. Just look at how God used him:

- Even as a young boy, Samuel gave God's message of judgment to Eli, inaugurating his service as a priest and prophet (1 Sam. 3).
- After Eli's death, Samuel became judge of God's people (1 Sam. 7). He traveled a yearly circuit to Bethel, Gilgal, and Mizpah to give leadership to Israel (vv. 15–17).
- Though initially reluctant to grant Israel's request for a king, Samuel anointed Saul as the first monarch of the nation (1 Sam. 8:4–8; 9:27–10:1).
- When God rejected rebellious Saul as king, Samuel announced prophetic judgment against Saul (1 Sam. 15:10–35).
- At Bethlehem, Samuel anointed David to take the place of Saul (1 Sam. 16:1–13).

Samuel died and was buried in his hometown of Ramah. The Bible says that "the Israelites gathered together and lamented for him, and buried him" (1 Sam. 25:1). It has been noted that Samuel points forward to the person of the Savior, the Lord Jesus Christ. The story of Samuel's conception and birth reveals the direct hand of God, just as with the conception and birth of Jesus. Other parallels can be found between Samuel's ministry as judge, prophet, and priest and the ministry of Christ.

Samuel, the son conceived in response to a desperate prayer, provided Hannah and Elkanah with a wonderful heritage—all because Hannah dared to call on God during her time of greatest need. Hannah had no idea that thousands of years later we would read her story and find the courage to bring our needs to the Lord in faith as she did. She teaches us that when we trust God in the daily struggles of life, we offer a legacy of faith to those who will follow us.

You may never dream of what God has in mind to answer your prayers as you bring your deepest needs to Him. In all of our needs, He is all we need.

SUGGESTED SCRIPTURE READING

Psalm 63

PRAYER GUIDE

Think about these questions as you pray:

- Are your needs driving you toward God, or away from Him?
- Has any need in your life seemed too great to bring to God? Are you willing now to ask God to meet that need?
- Are you willing to accept God's answer to your problem, no matter what that answer may be?

- Have you looked beyond your immediate desire to see that your greatest need is Him?
- Are you seeking to praise God morning and night as you wait on Him to meet your needs?

Part 3

DAVID'S PRAYER OF RESTORATION

Principles for Praying with Purpose
God's people can fail.
God purifies through prayer.
God can restore failures.
God's mercy removes guilt.
Prayer can prevent failure.

Day 15

Praying Through a Failure

He seemed invincible.

Mind-bendingly tough answers like Leif Ericson, Johannes Kepler, George III, and Ecuador (the clue: "A Spanish dictionary defines it as 'Circulo maximo que equidista de los polos de la Tierra'") seemed easy to him. Topics like geography, history, and even Bible gave him no trouble at all.

Every opponent who dared to stand against him stood by helplessly as he relentlessly responded. Given answer after answer on the television game show *Jeopardy!* he could come up with the right question (the point of the game). It appeared that no one could beat champion Ken Jennings. Then, after seventy-five shows, two thousand seven hundred correct responses and more than $2.5 million in winnings, Jennings—a software engineer from Salt Lake City who became a smiling, brainy pop-culture hero during his winning streak—finally put down his buzzer.

On November 30, 2004, host Alex Trebek gave the answer: "Most of this firm's seventy thousand seasonal white-collar employees work only four months a year."

Ken responded, "What is FedEx?"

His opponent, Nancy Zerg, answered (correctly), "What is H & R Block?"[1]

Some television viewers groaned when their champion failed. Others cheered that someone had finally beaten Jennings. Just about everyone agreed, though, that the question he missed was by no means the most difficult he had faced.

King David of Israel found himself in much greater jeopardy.

He once had seemed invincible. As a shepherd boy, he defended his sheep from lions and bears. As a young man, he killed the giant Goliath with a leather sling and one smooth stone. Later his army conquered tens of thousands of Israel's enemies on the battlefields. He spent years in the wilderness, on the run from the crazed, jealous King Saul. As king of Israel, he fought more battles and won more victories.

Intellectually, politically, militarily, artistically, spiritually—you name it—David had been a champion on every front.

Then, when it looked as though his feet were planted firmly, he fell—horribly and tragically. David's spiritual failure rocked his soul to the core.

We might think that the thing that caused David to fail was by no means the most difficult test he faced. The truth is, though, that every believer—no matter how strong we are or how great our track record may look—is vulnerable to temptation, sin, and failure.

There's a momentous lesson to be learned from the story of David's reaction to his failure. David did not fail to seek God after he failed. As we examine his story, we will discover how God can empower us to call on Him during our seasons of failure.

SCRIPTURE READING

1 Corinthians 10:12–13

PRAYER GUIDE

As you pray . . .

- thank God for His grace that is able to keep you from temptation.
- praise the Lord for His promise to restore you when you have sinned.
- ask that God will teach you from the example of David both how to avoid spiritual failure and how to seek His forgiveness when you fail.

Day 16

When All Systems Fail

But the thing that David had done
displeased the LORD. (2 Sam. 11:27b)

Whenever a man or woman fails to
walk with God, they walk on the
edge of an abyss.
　　　　　—Haddon W. Robinson[1]

God's people can fail.

This chapter could have opened with a different sentence, such as, "God's people make mistakes," but those words aren't strong enough. Wearing a polka-dot shirt with checkered pants and a striped jacket is a mistake, as is asking for a price check at the "Everything's a Dollar" store or ordering barbecued ribs dripping with sauce on a first date. But none of these mistakes break the heart of a holy God. The issues with which we're going to deal in the pages that follow are far more serious than "mistakes."

The statement, "Believers can commit horrible sin," gets a little closer to the issue at hand. We're about to examine a case study of a scandalous sin and its more ghastly cover-up. But even talking about committing sin doesn't capture the dark depths of reality here.

While we understand that God's people make mistakes and that believers can commit horrible sin, we're looking at the most notorious episode in the life of David, who experienced a complete collapse in his personality, his morality, his ethics, his decision making, and his relationship with God. David's adultery with Bathsheba and murder of Uriah reveal a total system failure that could only be remedied by earnest prayer.

AFTER GOD'S OWN HEART

The prophet Samuel described David as a man after God's own heart (1 Sam. 13:14). Such was God's favor on David's life and the general tenor of David's relationship with his Lord. David's heart beat in time with God's.

Watching over his father's sheep, David had learned to depend on God, and God blessed him in wonderful ways. Haddon Robinson lists the extraordinary natural gifts God gave David, imaginatively describing him as "a boy with a 160 IQ, with the hand and eye coordination of a Michael Jordan, with the musical ability of an Andrew Lloyd Webber, and the poetic genius of a Shakespeare."[2]

David's talents and bravery—empowered by the anointing hand of God—eventually and providentially brought David to a position of leadership over Israel. As Israel's king, David succeeded in every way imaginable:

- He began his military career by killing the champion of the enemy army, a feared giant.
- He built an army that all his enemies admired and was never defeated on the battlefield.
- He led for two decades with never-equaled success in national politics and international affairs. He surrounded himself with capable, trustworthy advisers.
- He enlarged the nation's boundaries significantly and created national wealth through increased world trade. He developed a strong national defense.

- He built a beautiful new palace and drafted plans for God's temple.

As he neared age fifty, David's résumé looked great. He had excelled in every task to which he set his hand. But something was happening underneath the surface in his life. Nathan, the prophet who advised David spiritually, missed the signs of budding arrogance. Joab, David's loyal but devious military commander, did not detect it, for he had the same problem. David himself likely was not even aware that his spiritual life had slipped as his outward success had reached its zenith.

WARNING SIGNS

The man after God's own heart had been coasting in his relationship with God. The king had lost his fervor and passion in worship. As a shepherd—looking out at the nighttime sky sparkling over Palestine—he had strummed his harp and sung countless songs of praise to the Lord. God's presence had been more real to David than the sound of the sheep nearby or the coolness of the breeze across his ruddy face. As the young leader of a band of vigilante outlaws hiding from King Saul's madness, David had to rely upon God as his Rock and Fortress.

But now, he was safe in a luxurious new palace. Israel still had to fight other nations, but his enemies were under control. He was in his stride—there seemed to be no challenge he could not manage. So, along the way, David had come to a point when he no longer felt his moment-by-moment dependence on God.

And there were ominous warning signs of impending disaster. The first sign was *callousness.* In Deuteronomy 17:16–17, long before David had taken the crown, God had established three stringent laws specifically to restrain kings of His people: "He shall not multiply horses for himself. . . . Neither shall he multiply wives for himself, lest his heart turn away; . . . nor shall he greatly multiply silver and gold for himself." Scripture says nothing about a cavalry or chariots in the army under Joab. He still trusted in God's strength to conquer his enemies. David doesn't seem to have been obsessed with gathering great treasure.

But in the matter of sexuality, David was very disobedient. "And David took more concubines and wives from Jerusalem, after he had come from Hebron" (2 Sam. 5:13). At that time, political alliances through marriage could be expedient, and David also had an issue with lust. His wives and mistresses increased in number, in callous disobedience to God.

Another warning sign was *complacency.* David crashed and burned morally because he was taking a break when he should have been fighting a battle. The story opens in 2 Samuel 11:1 with the background comment, "It happened in the spring of the year, at the time when kings go out to battle, that David sent Joab and his servants with him, and all Israel. . . . But David remained at Jerusalem." David had become a lazy, complacent king. At the time of year when kings led their armies out to war, he stayed home and sent Joab, even though God had chosen David to command.

A final warning sign was *carelessness.* The Bible indicates that David arose from his bed one evening and began to walk on the roof of his house. The roof was flat, like a patio, and he could see and hear things from all sides as he strolled around at dusk.

Maybe he heard the splash of water as servants filled a large stone basin. Perhaps Bathsheba was singing a dance song. Was she deliberately tempting the king? Probably not, for the roof was where people did such things as bathe. But she *was* perhaps being immodest in easy sight of the palace. Whatever initially attracted his attention, David soon found himself dangerously gazing at his neighbor's wife as she bathed. God's Word says, "From the roof he saw a woman bathing, and the woman was very beautiful to behold" (2 Sam. 11:2b).

How did David fall so far? David didn't fall far at all. He was very close to the bottom when he fell. Most of us don't dive into sin so much as we take the slide into the pool. Warning signs that we're slipping away from the Lord appear long before the plunge.

David's warning signs are the same for us today. You enjoy no closer walk with God than did David. Nor are you less susceptible to failure. Ask yourself:

- *Have you become callous?* The one who becomes spiritually insensitive finds it easy to disobey and then make excuses to justify sin.
- *Are you complacent?* You are entering hazardous spiritual territory when enthusiasm for seeking and doing God's will diminishes.
- *Have you become careless in your devotion to God?* Neglecting to guard your eyes, ears, mouth, and hands takes you into the danger zone.

HOW SIN MULTIPLIES

The Bible does not tell how willingly Bathsheba came when the king sent for her. But not many days after Bathsheba returned home, she sent the message, "I am with child" (2 Sam. 11:5). As he read Bathsheba's note, panic gripped David's body. What would he do?

Someone has said, "To err is human, and to try to cover it up is even more human." Instead of going to God with his sin, David put into motion an elaborate scheme to conceal his sin. He contacted Joab and asked for Uriah—Bathsheba's husband—to be called in from the battlefield and sent to the palace in Jerusalem. When Uriah appeared before David, the king asked him for an update on the war. After receiving Uriah's report, he dismissed his soldier and told him to go home.

As Uriah left his presence, David breathed a sigh of relief, thinking, "He'll go to see Bathsheba, and when the baby comes, he'll think it's his." Imagine David's shock the next day when he discovered that Uriah would not spend an intimate night with his wife while Israel's soldiers were camped out in the open battlefields. Instead, the faithful soldier had slept at the door of the king's house. David asked Uriah to stay a few more days, and even got him drunk, but nothing would break Uriah's loyalty to his king, his nation, and the Lord.

Finally, David sent Uriah back to the army, carrying an order for his own death. David had not thought it would come to this, but he surely reasoned that Uriah had given him no other option. The letter instructed Joab to "set Uriah in the forefront of the hottest battle, and retreat from him, that he may be struck down and die" (2 Sam. 11:15). Joab read the message and obeyed. He marched the armies of Israel to an indefensible position by the walls of the city they were attacking. Uriah, and probably others, were needlessly struck down as a result. Commander Joab sent back word that Uriah had died in the battle.

Bathsheba mourned for the minimum socially accepted period, then hurried to marry David before the baby was born.

David had now accumulated a substantial list of crimes: Coveting his neighbor's wife. Adultery with Bathsheba. Deception and betrayal against Uriah. Murder. More deception against the national conscience. David alone knew the full extent of his sin. Bathsheba knew about the adultery, but she might or might not have guessed that her husband had been killed at David's order. Joab knew David's scheme against Uriah, and he probably guessed the rest. Surely rumors flew about the kingdom, but David technically had succeeded. He had sinned, concealed his sin, and gotten everything he wanted. It looked like a perfect crime, except that "the thing that David had done displeased the LORD" (2 Sam. 11:27).

"YOU ARE THE MAN"

Though we might picture Nathan as a white-bearded, bony-fingered spokesman for God, the prophet may have been a younger man than King David. He appeared on the scene long after David came to power. He had helped David put together plans for the temple and then advised him that God planned for David's son to build it instead. Surely Nathan knew David's heart for God as well as anyone. He knew the king's lovely songs of praise. He observed how David sought God in his decisions.

So when God told Nathan of the king's crimes, the prophet must have been grieved. Then Nathan confronted David head-on. Nathan's message to David is a model for godly confrontation. He began by telling David a story: A rich man and a poor man lived in the same city. The poor man had only one possession, but he regarded it as precious—his lamb. When a hungry traveler came to the rich man's house, instead of taking from his own large flock, he stole and butchered the poor man's lamb.

Nathan had barely finished the story when David exploded, "That man should be put to death! He should restore four times what he took from his poor neighbor." Regarding this account, Alan Redpath remarks, "Have you observed that when you excuse sin in your own life, you become very critical of it in other people?"[3] Though David had rationalized his adultery and murder, he had no mercy for a sheep thief.

However, as soon as David's words of harsh judgment left his lips, he heard Nathan's dramatic pronouncement: "You are the man" (2 Sam. 12:7).

So much for the indirect approach.

If the rich man in the story had sinned against God, David must understand that he himself had sinned. God had blessed David with so much, and was willing to give him even more. Yet David had taken the wife of Uriah by violence and murder. His own household would lift hands in violence against him because of his sin. Other men would rape his wives, shaming him in front of the whole nation.

Nathan was effective in confronting David because of four things, according to a commentator: First, he came to the king with *absolute truth* from God. Second, he confronted with the *right timing*, only after God sent him. Third, Nathan tackled David's problem with *wise wording*, helping the king identify his own sin through a parable. Fourth, Nathan showed *fearless courage* in saying, "You are the man!"[4]

David's response was swift and complete. After more than a year of scheming and selfish wickedness, he broke down before the prophet: "So David said to Nathan, 'I have sinned against the LORD'" (2 Sam. 12:13a). He offered no more rationalizing and no excuses. He didn't even ask to be spared his punishment, which normally would have been the death penalty. He simply admitted, "I have sinned against the LORD."

Nathan responded to that confession, "The LORD also has put away your sin; you shall not die" (v. 13b). He would pay such consequences, though, that he might have preferred stoning. He drank a bitter cup of repercussion. Bathsheba's newborn son died. Turmoil wrecked David's household. Amnon, one of David's sons, raped Tamar, a half sister. Another son, Absalom, would avenge Tamar's death by killing Amnon. Then Absalom started a civil war to take the throne from David. Later, David's son Adonijah tried the same thing. David's moral and spiritual influence in Israel would never be what it had been.

Even so, God forgave and restored David.

WE CANNOT WAIT

Those living in the United States at the time will remember September 11, 2001. We watched in stunned disbelief as airliners exploded and the World Trade Center towers fell. The images were nightmarish, like some disaster movie script run amuck in real life. After the 9/11 attacks, we began asking, "What went wrong? What systems failed so these attacks could happen?"

When asked about the failures, the national security advisor to President George W. Bush, Condoleezza Rice, observed that those charged to stop attacks must find and stop them 100 percent of the time in order to succeed, while the terrorists only have to succeed once: "That is why we must address the source of the problem. We must stay on the offensive to find and defeat the terrorists wherever they live, hide, and plot around the world. If we learned anything from September 11th, it is that we cannot wait while dangers gather."[5]

The same is true spiritually. Satan attacks us each day. He only has to succeed once to devastate our personal lives, our families, and our churches. We have to stay on the offensive; we cannot wait while dangers gather. God says, "Let him who thinks he stands take heed lest he fall" (1 Cor. 10:12).

As David failed, so can every child of God. But by God's grace and through earnest prayer, we can stay on the alert against failure. He is able to keep us from falling.

SUGGESTED SCRIPTURE READING

1 John 1:5–10

PRAYER GUIDE

Seek God by . . .

- praising Him for being your light.
- asking Him to reveal sin in your life, so that you can be truthful with God.
- thanking Him for the accountability other Christians can give.
- asking Him to make your heart sensitive, so you do not deceive yourself.
- confessing your sin.
- thanking Him for forgiveness and cleansing through Jesus's death on the cross.
- asking Him to help you keep sins confessed and fellowship open.

Day 17

COMING CLEAN WITH GOD

> Wash me thoroughly from my
> iniquity, And cleanse me from my
> sin. (Ps. 51:2)

> Lord, wash, and wash, and wash
> again, till the last stain is gone, and
> not a trace of my defilement is left!
> —Charles Haddon Spurgeon[1]

God purifies through prayer.

It took four hours to clean him. He had not taken a bath in ten years, and his neighbors were sickened by the odor. So, four villagers swooped on the fifty-two-year-old man in rural western Kenya, tied him with a rope so that he couldn't get away, stripped him, and scrubbed him clean. His body had to be scoured with sand to remove a thick layer of filth. *Kenya Times* reported that after his bath the man—who was a bachelor—promised to wash once a day and hoped soon to find a wife.[2]

Going ten years without bathing sounds pretty disgusting, but how about one of God's people going for nearly a year without spiritual cleaning? That's what David did after he sinned with

Bathsheba and murdered Uriah. There was a span of ten to twelve months between the time that David began this episode of sin and the time he confessed. It is hard to imagine how a man who had enjoyed such a deep relationship with God could continue so long with unconfessed sin in his life. During that period, the stench of David's disobedience was repulsive to God's nostrils.

It was grace that sent Nathan to confront David. Immediately, David sought and received forgiveness. David's words of repentance to Nathan are brief. He simply said, "I have sinned against the LORD" (2 Sam. 12:13a). In Psalm 51, however, God's Word presents one of David's prayers related to this time. There, with stirring language, David describes the filth of his sin, the urgency of his repentance, and the hope for God's forgiveness.

THE FOUNDATIONS FOR OUR CLEANSING

When we fail, we can come to God, knowing He will restore us because of Jesus Christ. We are forgiven because of who God is and what He has done in Christ, not because of who we are. When David sought God's cleansing, he understood forgiveness depended completely on God. "Have mercy upon me, O God, according to Your lovingkindness; according to the multitude of Your tender mercies, blot out my transgressions" (Ps. 51:1).

Twice David used the phrase that is translated "according to." Those words speak of the basis on which David dared to ask for forgiveness. Forgiveness rested on two foundational truths about the Lord.

First, David relied on God's unfailing love. He asked for God to show mercy according to His lovingkindness. The Hebrew term refers to God's everlasting and steadfast love. God sent Christ and forgives His redeemed people through Christ because His love for us is unceasing. He never fails to love us, even when we have failed miserably.

Second, David relied on God's great mercy. He anticipated the work of Christ as he prayed for his sins to be blotted out according to the "multitude" of God's "tender mercies." The expression translated "tender mercies" captures the warmth of God's compassion toward His people. Though He never indulges our sin, He is able to forgive far beyond what we could ever imagine. God is not a "penny-pincher," doling out mercy drop by drop. Instead, He pours out His mercy abundantly to cleanse and forgive.

Some people arrogantly believe that they deserve God's forgiveness or that their prominence in God's kingdom excuses them from the penalty of their sin: "I know God will let me off the hook for this. After all, I'm a pretty good person on the whole. I've just messed up in this one area. I deserve another chance." Even more presumptuous, a leader in the church might assume, "God is counting on me. If I go down, His kingdom will suffer. It's in His best interest to forgive me."

God does not forgive us because we deserve it. Neither does He forgive us because He needs us or owes us. He owes us nothing for sin except eternal death. Anyone who thinks he or she deserves God's cleansing absolutely will not obtain it. A repentant heart is never an arrogant heart.

We don't know what David was telling himself during all those months without confessing his sin. He may have excused himself because . . .

- "I've been a champion for the Lord. My body is scarred from the battles I have fought for Him. Do a few days of weakness override a lifetime of service?"
- "God has used me in the past. People even praise Him with psalms I wrote. Surely He'll overlook my sin this time."
- "I'm the spiritual leader of God's people. They look to me as an example. I need to keep this sin covered up out of love and respect for them."

Whatever flimsy rationalizations David might have used, he abandoned them all. "Have mercy upon me, O God!" he prayed.

God calls us to pray the same way. He wants us to step off the rickety bridge of our own excuses and self-righteousness and step onto the sure foundation of His character. It takes humility and faith to abandon our shabby little structure, but it's the way to take hold of the forgiveness a believer has in Christ. With one foot resting on the rock of God's unfailing love and the other foot planted on the boulder of the Lord's compassion, we can plead with God for cleansing, and know that He will forgive.

HE IS ABLE

Based on God's love and mercy, David asked for God to forgive his sin. Pay close attention to the words of his request. David's language reveals some very important things about how God views our sin and how He is able to cleanse us.

"Blot out my transgressions. Wash me thoroughly from my iniquity, and cleanse me from my sin" (Ps. 51:1b–2). David asked God for three things: (1) for his transgressions to be blotted out; (2) for his iniquity to be washed away; and (3) for his life to be cleansed of sin. David uses a distinct word for sin in each of the three phrases, as well as a distinct word to describe how God deals with sin.

"Blot out my transgressions." A "transgression" is a deliberate act of rebellion. As king, David knew about rebels who broke laws deliberately. He had reviewed many legal documents describing the violence and wickedness of these criminals. David understood that his sin was an illegal act—a crime against God. He had willfully broken God's laws. By asking God to blot out his transgression, David was saying, "God, erase this offense from my permanent record. Give me a clean report once again."

"Wash me thoroughly from my iniquity." "Iniquity" is guilt—not just guilty feelings but objective and provable guiltiness before God. David wasn't saying, "God help me not to feel so bad about the things I've done." Instead, he asked God to wash away the real dirtiness that caused his shame. The Bible sometimes compares repentance with the washing of dirty clothes, but David knew his iniquity was far

worse than dirt on garments. He had been bathing in the deep-hued dye of sin. The stain had penetrated far beyond the outer surfaces of David's life. Guilt had seeped into his soul and was corrupting his heart. He needed more than to be washed from his iniquity. He needed to be washed *thoroughly*—in-depth and long enough so that every stain was gone.

"Cleanse me from my sin." His final plea for forgiveness borrows from the language of the tabernacle and its sacrifices, which looked forward to the coming of a sacrifice adequate to the infinite offense of sin before God. Worshippers who came into God's presence had to be ceremonially clean. David knew that as long as he fell short of God's standard, he had no possibility of connection with God. For the past year, David's prayers had been empty words. The songs of praise he tried to offer had turned into mockery and insults in God's ears. When David pretended to worship, God saw nothing but sin's defiling mark. So, he prayed to be cleansed.

There's something especially encouraging about these petitions. David's requests remind us that we do not need to give up hope when we fail. Because of Christ, spiritual failures need not be everlasting defeats. And God provides a way of dealing with even the worst failures in the lives of His children.

- When we commit transgressions, He blots out the record against us.
- When we are guilty of iniquity, He washes away the stain.
- When we sin, He is justified to purify us.

No sin we bring to God is beyond the reach of His mercy, love, and forgiveness. God is willing to cleanse the sin of any person who comes to confess and look to Christ's sacrifice. He tells us, "He who covers his sins will not prosper, but whoever confesses and forsakes them will have mercy" (Prov. 28:13). As David continues his prayer, we can see how he confessed his sin to God.

AGREEING WITH GOD

We have become experts in the art of making unapologetic apologies. You may have heard some people's lame efforts at making amends without admitting guilt, whether the culprit is a politician trying to avoid removal from office, a celebrity attempting to prevent a public relations fiasco, or a corporation staving off a potential lawsuit.

These fake apologies sound something like this:

- "We are sincerely sorry for any mistakes that may have been made."
- "I offer my deepest apologies if my actions have offended anyone."
- "I deeply regret if anyone has been hurt by the alleged offenses."

Do you hear the hypocritical undertones of these "apologies"? Behind the "I'm sorry" is an arrogant attitude that says, "As far as I'm concerned, I didn't do one thing wrong. Even if I did, it's none of your business. Anyone offended by what I've done is prudish and overly sensitive to begin with. Now, here's your cotton-picking apology. Get off my back!"

Some of our prayers aren't very different from those sham apologies. Instead of coming clean about our sin, we vaguely pray, "Lord, if I've done anything wrong (and I'm pretty sure I haven't), forgive me." This type of empty prayer has even been set to music. There's an awful old hymn that goes,

> If I have wounded any soul today,
> If I have caused one foot to go astray,
> If I have walked in my own willful way,
> Dear Lord, forgive.
> (C. Maude Battersby, "An Evening
> Prayer," c. 1911)

Be careful not to let the word *if* creep into your confessions to God. There's a place for asking God to forgive unintentional sins, and there are sins we commit each day of which we are unaware. In another prayer of David, he asks to be cleansed from secret faults (Ps. 19:12). Praying for cleansing for secret sins, though, involves God revealing those sins to us. Once we *know* what our sins are, we should confess those sins specifically and truthfully. It's not enough just to say, "Lord, forgive me of any sins I may have committed," or "God, if I've hurt You or someone else today, forgive me."

David didn't make excuses. He did not paint a rosy picture of his wickedness. He didn't blame someone else. With real repentance and genuine sorrow, he owned up to his sin:

> For I acknowledge my transgressions, and my sin is always before me. Against You, You only, have I sinned, and done this evil in Your sight—that You may be found just when You speak, and blameless when You judge. Behold, I was brought forth in iniquity, and in sin my mother conceived me. Behold, You desire truth in the inward parts, and in the hidden part You will make me to know wisdom. (Psalm 51:3–6)

Notice what David acknowledges.

He confesses that he has sinned. By saying, "I acknowledge my transgressions, and my sin is always before me," David agrees with God that he has sinned. That kind of acknowledgement is at the heart of real confession. God tells us, "If we confess our sins, He is faithful and just to forgive us our sins and to cleanse us from all unrighteousness" (1 John 1:9). Confessing means saying the same thing about our sins that God says about them. Human nature tempts us to play down our own wickedness. Instead of saying we lied, we say **we stretched the truth.** We didn't *steal*; we *borrowed*. We didn't *commit adultery*; we had *an affair of the heart*. Genuine confession only occurs when we say, "God, I'm not glossing over what I've done. I have sinned. I have done wickedness."

He confesses that he has offended God. David prayed, "Against You,

You only, have I sinned, and done this evil in Your sight." David was not denying that his sin had damaged other people. He had ruined Bathsheba's reputation, destroyed her marriage, and caused her the grief of burying an infant son. He had brought Uriah's life to a violent and bloody end. He had deceived and misled the entire nation of Israel, who trusted him to be an honorable leader. But behind these interpersonal wrongs, David's real sin was that he offended God. Sin wounds His love. Sin violates His law. Though confession often includes seeking forgiveness from other people, we must confess our sin to God before we can make things right with anyone else.

He confesses that he deserves punishment. David said that God was just when He spoke and blameless when He judged. David accepted the temporal consequences for his sin. He had been told that the child conceived in adultery with Bathsheba would die, that his children would dishonor him, and that his wives would be taken from him. Nathan the prophet had told David that these things would happen (2 Sam. 12:10–11, 14), and they all did. But David was not focused on escaping the repercussions of what he had done. Instead, he was seeking a restored relationship with the Lord. David admitted that he was guilty as charged and deserved whatever judgment he received.

By His grace, God may keep believers from experiencing the earthly consequences for our sin. Certainly, when lost people trust Jesus Christ to save them from sin, God's grace delivers them from eternity in hell. But praying, "Lord, don't let me get in trouble for committing this sin," will not bring forgiveness. Nor will praying, "God, don't let me go to hell when I die," bring a lost person the gift of eternal life. Genuine confession always aims at being cleansed of sin rather than being excused from punishment.

He accepts responsibility for what he has done. As he prayed, "Behold, I was brought forth in iniquity, and in sin my mother conceived me," David acknowledged that he had been a sinner from conception. Sin was part of his nature, and he bore the blame for what he had done. When we sin, we may be tempted to point the finger at other people, or our circumstances, or Satan, or even God, and deny our own guilt. Cleansing only comes, however, when we say, "Lord, I blame myself for this sin. Please forgive me."

He confesses that God has something better for him. David continued his confession by telling the Lord, "Behold, You desire truth in the inward parts, and in the hidden part You will make me to know wisdom." David acknowledged that God didn't intend for him to continue in the life of falsehood and foolishness that he had been living. Instead, the king knew that God wanted him to live a life marked by God's truth and wisdom.

A CLEAN GLASS

Two ladies sat down for lunch in a restaurant. The waiter came and asked them what they wanted to drink.

The first lady said, "I'll have iced tea."

The second lady said, "I'll have the same thing, and make sure the glass is clean."

A moment later the waiter returned. "Two teas," he said, "and which one of you wanted the clean glass?"

The answer, of course, is that no one wants anything but a clean glass. And God wants believers in Christ to be clean vessels as well.

Unconfessed sin will not keep a believer out of heaven. Speaking of those whom He saved, Jesus said, "I give them eternal life, and they shall never perish; neither shall anyone snatch them out of My hand" (John 10:28). If Jesus has truly saved you, you are saved forever.

What unconfessed sin *will* do is to keep you from having the benefit of a close fellowship with the Lord. Sins that go unconfessed rob believers of God's peace and joy. Unconfessed sin will deprive you of being able to worship and serve Christ. When we are spiritually unclean, we will not experience God's best for our lives.

We want to stay clean. That's why we confess sin in prayer.

SUGGESTED SCRIPTURE

Psalm 51:1–6

PRAYER GUIDE

When believers sin, we can find God's cleansing through confession and repentance. In a prayer of confession . . .

- thank God for His mercy and loving-kindness.
- name the sins you have committed, without excuses.
- ask God to blot out your transgressions.
- ask God to wash away the stain of your iniquity.
- ask God to purify you.
- thank God for His forgiving grace through Jesus Christ.

MOVING FORWARD FROM FAILURE

Create in me a clean heart, O God,
And renew a steadfast spirit within
me. (Ps. 51:10)

I have trembled and failed again and
again, but God has never failed.
—J. Hudson Taylor[1]

*G*od can restore failures.

Michael Jordan appears in one of my favorite television commercials.

The camera follows Jordan as he walks toward the locker room. We watch him moving in slow-motion, with a voice-over that says, "I've missed more than nine thousand shots in my career. I've lost almost three hundred games. Twenty-six times I've been trusted to take the game-winning shot—and missed. I've failed."

Arguably Michael Jordan has been history's greatest basketball athlete, yet he says, "I've failed." Those words are extremely hard for an athlete to say. Those words are hard for anyone to say. Failure is disappointing and heartbreaking. It lets the air out of the ego and takes the sheen off our reputation. Who wants to admit to failure?

Jordan admits, "I've failed," but at the end of the commercial, he expands on his failure: "I've failed over and over again in my life. And that is why I succeed."

Is there success and purpose on the other side of failure? In Jesus Christ, there is. God's redeeming power can snatch spiritual victory from the jaws of defeat. He possesses an awesome ability to restore us when we have failed. David discovered this glorious truth as he prayed, and so can we.

NEVER THE SAME

"I don't see how it can ever be the same," she said.

She was seventeen, an excellent student, a really sweet young lady . . . and she was three months pregnant. Her youth pastor had to agree that she could never go back to what had been, though he didn't want to say it out loud. Neither the head pastor or his wife knew exactly how to respond. They loved this girl, and they wanted to help her, but they were shocked. She was a church kid. Never missed Sunday school. Went on mission trips each summer. She had meant it when she pledged to remain sexually pure until marriage. Now this.

She made no excuses for herself. She knew she had sinned. She had already sought and found God's forgiveness. Her father and mother, though hurt, had been understanding. Even so, she felt like she had sentenced herself to a future filled with regret.

With tears in her eyes, she repeated, "I don't see how things can ever be the same."

Other people in similar situations have voiced the same thoughts. We fail. We confess. We are forgiven. But we wonder, *Can life ever be the way it was before?* The answer is that our sins have consequences that linger even after we're forgiven. But though life may not be the same, God has a plan for our future that takes into account our failures.

Your failures never take God by surprise. Omniscient, He saw them coming. His intention is for you to live within His will, but as you confess and receive forgiveness, He continues to work out His purpose in your life.

Consider what happened in the garden of Eden. The first man and woman were living in a perfect world. Their futures were settled; they would live forever in unbroken fellowship with the God who made them. Everything would be endlessly wonderful. Then sin entered in. They disobeyed God. Death came into the human race. They were expelled from the garden. They had it all, and they lost it all.

Did Adam and Eve's sin in the garden cause God to declare a state of emergency in heaven? Was God running around in circles, panicked, wondering what to do next? No, He already had the plan in place, so that He could immediately promise to send His Son to redeem the world from sin (Gen. 3:15; Titus 1:2). He chose to use evil to accomplish His good purpose—His glory through our redemption in Jesus Christ.

In the same way, once we confess and are cleansed of our sin, God will work His arrangement for our future, in spite of our failure. For believers in Christ, our failures do not have to be fatal or final.[2]

After his sin with Bathsheba, David must have wondered:

- "Lord, will You use me again?"
- "Will Your people ever look to me as a spiritual leader?"
- "Will I again compose a song of praise that comes straight from You?"

Even as David prayed for forgiveness, God was answering *yes* to all of those questions. His prayer in Psalm 51 is itself of great use as a guide for repentance, a testimony to God's forgiving power, and a song of praise for restoration.

HOW GOD RESTORES

In the early part of Psalm 51, David confessed his sin and asked for God's forgiveness. As the psalm progresses, David begins to ask God for restoration. His petitions show how well David understood the depths of God's ability to restore those who fail. His requests reveal five areas of restoration God accomplishes as He forgives.

Restoring our purity. David prays, "Purge me with hyssop, and I shall be clean; wash me, and I shall be whiter than snow" (Ps. 51:7). Hyssop was a leafy plant that the priests used to sprinkle blood and water on those who had been cleansed from physical defilement. If a leper, for instance, was healed, he had to be washed with hyssop before he was considered clean (Lev. 14:1–8). The children of Israel used hyssop to apply the blood of the lamb on their lintels and doorposts at the Passover (Exod. 12:22). To be purged with hyssop, then, meant to be declared pure and delivered from death. Through God's purging, David knew that he would be washed whiter than snow.

David continued asking for God to restore his purity, praying that God would hide His face from David's sins, and blot out all his iniquities (Ps. 51:9). Then, he made this request: "Create in me a clean heart, O God, and renew a steadfast spirit within me" (Ps. 51:10). The Hebrew word for "create" means "to originate." The term is used in the Bible of God as the source of something. For instance, when God created the heavens and the earth, He did something only He can do. David knew that God alone could create a new heart in him. In David's language, the heart represented the very core of a person. The conscience, the inner self, and human spirit are all encompassed by the word *heart.* David was saying, "God make my heart anew. Make it clean as it once was. Make my spirit steadfast and whole once again."

Forgiveness transforms the inner personality of the believer. We are born in sin, but we are reborn with a pure heart when we place our faith in Christ. And then, when we sin as believers and seek God's cleansing, He purifies us and makes us like new once more.

Restoring our closeness. The request, "Do not cast me away from Your presence, and do not take Your Holy Spirit from me" (Ps. 51:11), is the heart cry of a runaway child who wants desperately to come back home. David remembered when he lived in close fellowship with the Lord. Now his mind reached back to recall the intimate bond that God forged with his young soul on the day Samuel had anointed him to be Israel's king. He knew that King Saul had been removed from kingship because of his disobedience to God. The Lord's Spirit had departed from him (1 Sam. 16:14). David begged God, "Don't banish me from Your presence because of my sin. Don't take away Your Spirit from me and remove me from leading Your people as You did Saul." Even before he had plunged into the depths of sin, David had lost a measure of his closeness with the Lord. God seemed thousands of miles away. David wanted to reestablish connection.

David lived in a time when the Holy Spirit came upon people at special times to empower them for special tasks. In Jesus Christ, the Holy Spirit indwells believers permanently from the moment of salvation (John 14:16). He seals us, marking us as God's possession until the day that Jesus returns (Eph. 1:13–14).

The Holy Spirit will never be taken away from a child of God. Even so, Christians do grieve God's Spirit and quench God's Spirit through our sin or resistance to His work (Eph. 4:30; 1 Thess. 5:19). We can be cast aside from serving. We can lose fellowship with God. Through confession and cleansing, God restores the full work of the Holy Spirit in our lives. He enables us to again walk in close communion with the God who indwells us by His Spirit.

Restoring our joy. In his prayer, David speaks of regaining joy through God's forgiveness. He knows that God alone is able to make the broken bones of his sorrow dance and rejoice before the Lord (Ps. 51:8). He asks God to take his lips, which had been closed in his backslidden condition, and to open them once more in praise (Ps. 51:15). As David came to God in prayer, he confessed that it had been a long time since he had known real joy and gladness.

Perhaps his strongest petition for renewed joy is "Restore to me the joy of Your salvation, and uphold me by Your generous Spirit"

(Ps. 51:12). David had lost his song, not his soul. He understood God's faithfulness and knew that his sin could not snatch him away from God's hand. Indeed, God's faithful hand had disciplined David in his sin. David's experience showed him, however, that the joy of his salvation had fled. He urgently wanted that joy to return.

No one who has been genuinely saved can continue in sin and enjoy it. When the Holy Spirit who lives inside of us becomes grieved, we will not be happy. We may look for distraction in business or more sin or even Christian activity—but deep down will be the restless sadness of living with unconfessed sin. The same Holy Spirit who becomes grieved over our sin is able to uphold and lift us out of sin's misery when we confess.

Restoring our testimony. When we are forgiven, we are able again to tell others about God's grace at work in our lives. In response to God's work of restoration, David prays, "Then I will teach transgressors Your ways, and sinners shall be converted to You. Deliver me from the guilt of bloodshed, O God, the God of my salvation, and my tongue shall sing aloud of Your righteousness" (Ps. 51:13–14). David anticipated the time when he would be able to teach other sinners about the grace and goodness of God, so that they would turn from their sins as well.

Restoring our acceptance. In the concluding verses of this psalm, David asks for a new acceptance as he offers sacrifices to God. He says, "You do not desire sacrifice, or else I would give it; You do not delight in burnt offering" (Ps. 51:16). All of the many bulls and goats offered on the altar would not please God as long as David continued in sin. Those rituals became empty without genuine repentance.

Instead, David recognized that the sacrifices that pleased God were "a broken spirit" and a "broken and a contrite heart" (Ps. 51:17). The words *broken* and *contrite* paint a picture of the heart that is acceptable to God. The Hebrew word translated "broken" refers to something violently shattered or broken into pieces. The word translated "contrite" comes from a root verb meaning "to crush."

A broken heart is the kind of heart Christ enters. As long as our hearts remain hardened, our defenses are up, and our wills remain braced, God will not do the work He wants to do in us. We are acceptable to Him only at the point of brokenness.

Praise God! When we are broken before Him, God can work in our lives once more. He forgives, restores, and begins anew to use us for His purposes.

SUCCESSFUL FAILURES

Some Christians are missing out on God's best for their lives because they think that, with the sin they have committed, it's too late. They believe God can never use them again. David's testimony is just one example of God's ability to take broken people and use them mightily. Think about some other successful failures.

Jonah received a clear word from God to go to Nineveh and preach, then ran as hard as he could in the opposite direction. God's grace pursued him, sending a storm to frustrate the rebellious prophet's escape and a giant fish to redirect his paths. After everything, "the word of the LORD came to Jonah the second time" (Jonah 3:1). God filled Jonah's mouth with a message that he proclaimed to the wicked people at Nineveh, and the entire city turned to the Lord.

Moses murdered an Egyptian overseer of the Hebrew slaves. Frightened for his life, Moses spent the next forty years living in a desert wilderness, thinking that his usefulness to God was finished. But the Lord used Moses to deliver His people from their Egyptian slave masters. In God's strength, Moses gave God's law to the Israelites and led them to the threshold of the Promised Land.

Simon Peter slept in Gethsemane when Jesus had asked for him to pray. Then, the foolhardy fisherman denied ever knowing the Lord he had sworn to defend to the death. After Jesus died, Peter surely felt it was all over for him. He had failed in the very thing he had vowed never to do. But, following His resurrection, the Lord Jesus took special care to again commission Peter. Peter went on to become a bold preacher of the gospel and a wise leader of the early church.

Other testimonies abound in Scripture from the lives of Rahab,

John Mark, and Saul of Tarsus. God is able to transform failures into successes.

SECOND CHANCES

Several years ago, I preached for several nights of evangelistic meetings in rural South Carolina. During the day I visited and spoke at a number of places with the pastor of the church. Each morning, we would get up before daylight and travel to the Good Samaritan Colony, a substance abuse center for men in Ruby, South Carolina. We joined the men after they had breakfast and before they began their daily work. These men—all of whom had failure and regret in their past—listened intently. They asked great questions, and prayed with fervency.

Near the end of the week, one of the leaders at the center took me on a tour of the facility. The colony had a huge furniture refinishing operation. My guide took me step-by-step through the process, as the men stripped off discolored finish from old pieces of furniture, repaired what was broken, and applied new stain and varnish. The products were more beautiful than most pieces of new furniture.

The man who was giving the tour had been a resident at the center before he was trained and came back to be a supervisor. As I admired an antique chest of drawers, he observed, "As we restore this furniture, it reminds us of what God is doing in us. We've all failed. But God gives us second chances."

God's grace is able to restore after failure.

SUGGESTED SCRIPTURE READING

Psalm 51:7–19

PRAYER GUIDE

After confessing sins,

- praise God for forgiving your sins and washing your defilement away.
- ask God to restore your joy and gladness.
- ask God to give you a clean heart and renew your spirit.
- praise God for your salvation.

Day 19

Guilt-Free Living

Blessed is he whose transgression
is forgiven, whose sin is covered.
(Ps. 32:1)

When I bring my sins to the Lord
Jesus He casts them into the depths
of the sea—forgiven and forgotten.
He also puts up a sign, "No Fishing
Allowed!"

—Corrie ten Boom[1]

God's mercy removes guilt.

During the spring of 1945, as the British army liberated the nation of Denmark from German occupation, Nazi officials filled ammunition boxes with files, weapons, uniforms, and other materials. The Germans dumped the waterproof boxes into Lake Ornso.

For nearly four decades, those boxes lay undisturbed in the lake's mud. Then, in late 1982, divers from the Danish navy discovered the large containers. Thinking the boxes might hold gold or some other treasure stolen by the Nazis, the divers worked to retrieve them.

While working at the site, the dive crew suddenly realized that someone was shooting at them. A couple of bullets came uncomfortably close. An investigation soon pointed to a man who had been an informer for the Nazis during the war. He wanted to keep those boxes—and the information they contained—on the bottom of the lake.[2]

Imagine the fear that man had been carrying for decades. Because of guilt over his past crimes, the man had spent countless days and nights patrolling that lake, worried that someone would unearth proof of his evil past.

DEEPWATER GUILT

Many people live every day with deepwater guilt. Constantly, they feel the weight of sins—some committed years ago—bearing down on their hearts. Guilt may cause all of us on occasion to lash out at others. It may bind our minds with worry and fear. Guilt can cause physical problems such as high blood pressure, heart disease, stomach ulcers, and headaches. But whatever the other results may be, guilt invariably keeps us from enjoying the joy, hope, and peace we are to experience in Christ.

But there's good news. God has made the way for us to live without guilt.

So far, we have seen King David's moral and spiritual failure. We watch with disgust and disappointment as he commits adultery with Bathsheba and then tries to cover up his sin to the point of plotting to kill Uriah. In Psalm 51, we witness David's repentance and observe how he poured himself out to God in prayer, seeking cleansing from the Lord.

Psalm 32 probably was written long after David's sin and restoration. The ancient Hebrew inscription calls this psalm a *maschil*. Though the specific meaning of that Hebrew term is unclear, most Bible scholars say a *maschil* is a song of contemplation or teaching. Reading Psalm 32, perhaps we can picture David sitting in a quiet place, many years after he failed and was forgiven, plucking the strings of the old harp he has played since his boyhood. With the raspy voice of an old man, he sings about what God has done in his life.

The unmistakable theme of David's song is God's ability to remove our guilt.

FINDING TRUE HAPPINESS

David begins this psalm by proclaiming, "Blessed is he whose transgression is forgiven, whose sin is covered. Blessed is the man to whom the LORD does not impute iniquity, and in whose spirit there is no deceit" (Ps. 32:1–2).

David's testimony is that God's forgiveness had brought an indescribable happiness to his life. Imagine meeting King David on the sidewalk in Jerusalem the day after he prayed for God to forgive him. For the first time in a year, he's walking with a spring in his step and a smile on his face. Can you see him whistling one of those beautiful songs he wrote, saying hello to everyone he meets?

When you see him, you ask, "How are you today, Your Majesty?"

With a broad grin and an enthusiastic voice, he answers, "I'm doing wonderfully. God is good!"

To be blessed is to be happy. Interestingly, the very first word in the book of Psalms is "blessed"—happy. "Blessed is the man," Psalm 1:1 says, "who walks not in the counsel of the ungodly." In that psalm, God declares that those who follow His paths are happy. Psalm 32 reminds us, however, that God's happiness and joy are available even after we have strayed from His righteousness. When God removes our guilt, He renews our gladness.

Psychiatrist Thomas Szasz offered a cynical definition of happiness, calling it "an imaginary condition, formerly attributed by the living to the dead, now by adults to children, and by children to adults."[3] But God's Word offers a greater hope than that. Believers can have real and lasting happiness.

We find happiness when our transgression is carried away. God says, "Blessed is he whose transgression is forgiven." "Transgression" is rebellion against God. David says that he is happy because his rebellion has been forgiven. The word *forgiven* can refer to carrying something away. For instance, the word is used to describe the way in which the priests carried the ark of the covenant through the wilderness (Exod. 25:14). *Forgiven* also can picture something being lifted up, as when Noah's ark was lifted up by the waters of the great flood (Gen. 7:17). When God forgives our transgressions, He lifts the burden of our rebellion from our shoulders and carries it far away. Through prayer and confession, the weight of sin is lifted.

We find happiness when our sin is covered. "Blessed is he . . . whose sin is covered." Sin is failure to reach God's goal for our lives. God covers those sins when we confess. He conceals and hides them, even from His own sight. Human efforts and energies can never hide our sin. In Proverbs 28:13, God tells us, "He who covers his sin will not prosper." We'll always be unsuccessful when we attempt to hide our own sins. But God has the supernatural ability to cover them when we confess.

We find happiness when our name is cleared. David writes, "Blessed is the man to whom the LORD does not impute iniquity." *Iniquity* points to the crookedness of David's character. His sin had created a debt that needed to be settled. An old gospel song captures this idea:

> There was a time on earth, when in the book of Heaven
> An old account was standing, for sins yet unforgiven.
> My name was at the top, and many things below,
> I went unto the Keeper, and settled long ago.
> Long ago—down on my knees; long ago—I settled it all.
> Yes, the old account was settled long ago!
> And the record's clear today, for He washed my sins away,
> When the old account was settled long ago.
> (Frank M. Graham, "The Old Account Was Settled," 1902)

When we seek God's forgiveness, He removes the iniquity that was on our record. Our name is cleared of the debts we once owed.

We find happiness when our spirit is cleansed. The passage continues,

"Blessed is the man . . . in whose spirit there is no deceit." David's life had become perverted by wickedness. Through His mercy, God removed that impurity. Instantly, David's guilt departed, the warfare between him and God ended, and the joy of the Lord characterized his life once again. God removed all the filth of David's sin.

God's forgiveness brings true happiness. Real joy comes when your relationship with God is right. When you are praying daily and keeping your heart clean before God, you will be a happy person.

GUILT MANAGEMENT?

The joy with which David opens this psalm differs greatly from the sad tune he had been moaning before he found God's forgiveness. During the year he had concealed his sin, David's heart sang in minor keys. "When I kept silent, my bones grew old through my groaning all the day long. For day and night Your hand was heavy upon me; my vitality was turned into the drought of summer" (Ps. 32:3–4).

God disciplines and corrects those He loves (Prov. 3:11–12). Just as a parent's punishing of a child is seldom pleasant, God's correction is painful. When David did not confess his sin, his bones grew old. He became weak physically. God's powerful hand of correction was heavy on him, drying up his strength as a pool of water evaporates in the hot summer sun. David's experience illustrates that physical health is closely related to spiritual well-being.

David's physical and spiritual misery came from his own stubborn resistance to admit his guilt. Perhaps he hoped that in time the shame in his conscience and God's painful discipline would go away. But the more he put off confessing, the worse his suffering became. That's always what happens when we try to manage our guilt rather than confessing our sin.

I once carpooled with a guy who had purchased a used sedan. The car ran well and looked great. There was just one problem: A red warning light on the dashboard blinked constantly. Something under the hood needed repair. For the first few weeks, I watched the light blink off and on. Then, one morning it was no longer flashing.

"So," I said, pointing to the dashboard, "I see you got your car fixed." He chuckled and said, "No, look a little closer."

Looking closely at the dashboard, it turned out that he had stuck a tiny piece of black tape over the warning light.

A guilty conscience is like that red warning light on the dashboard. When it starts flashing, you can either deal with the trouble, or cover up the light. Attempting to cover up the warning signal of guilt is managing guilt rather than allowing God to fix it.

Some people manage guilt by drowning it. Immersion in food, drugs and alcohol, entertainment, hobbies, work, or even church activities can make us forget about our guilt. Guilty people try to escape dealing with their past sins by filling their lives with other things.

People also try to manage guilt by deflecting it. In the garden of Eden, Adam blamed Eve for his sin, and then Eve blamed the serpent. Today, people play the same blame game, redirecting their guilt to their parents, their environment, their background, or to some other person or thing.

Other people manage guilt by denying it. Secular society rejects the category of moral absolutes. For most people most of the time, there are no ultimate standards of right and wrong. As people lose their respect for a moral standard that finds its authority in God's Word, they can easily talk themselves out of feeling guilty.[4]

For example, among couples that live together without being married, an increasing number identify themselves as evangelical Christians. Men and women who at least superficially identify themselves with the people of God are living in relationships of continual disobedience to God. Most of them understand enough about the Bible to know that God prohibits sex outside of marriage in strong terms (e.g., Gal. 5:19–21; Heb. 13:4). They continue in a sinful lifestyle, though, because they either deny that what they are doing is sin or because they think God's standards have changed.

Whether the sin is sex outside of marriage, lying, stealing, anger, or violence—we're in a hazardous place when we deny our guilt before God. Sooner or later, every method we use to manage our guilt will fail. Guilt cannot be managed; it must be removed.

LIFTING THE BURDEN

Two men were on trial in San Diego Superior Court, charged with armed robbery. The prosecutor was questioning an eyewitness:

"Were you at the scene when the robbery took place?" The witness answered, "Yes."

"And you saw a vehicle leave at a high rate of speed?" Again came the answer, "Yes."

"And did you observe the occupants?" "Yes," the eyewitness said. "Two men."

"And are those two men present in court today?"

At this point the two defendants sealed their fate. They raised their hands.[5]

To experience God's mercy, we have to raise our hands and say, "I'm guilty." Psalm 32:5 reveals David's mind-set as he declared his guilt, as well as God's response to David's confession: "I acknowledged my sin to You, and my iniquity I have not hidden. I said, 'I will confess my transgressions to the LORD,' and You forgave the iniquity of my sin." Once David made up his mind to acknowledge his sins, to uncover his iniquity, and to confess his transgressions, God lifted his burden. The guilt of the sin that separated David from God was laid on Christ and gone from David's heart.

Confession and forgiveness do not change history. David and others endured pain because of the sin he had committed. A baby died. His children rebelled. Relationships suffered.

Nevertheless, even as David experienced the aftermath of his sin, he knew that things were right once again with the Lord. God took the weight of sin away from David's shoulders. God can do the same for us.

WHAT GOD DOES WITH OUR SINS

Rosalind Goforth served for many years as a missionary in China alongside her husband, Jonathan. She paid a great price in service to Jesus, leaving behind family and friends and the comforts of home in order tell the Chinese about the grace of Jesus. Nevertheless, for many years, Rosalind felt the weight of a burden of sin. Though she labored for Christ diligently, she nursed private feelings of spiritual failure. She felt shameful and dirty. She prayed for forgiveness, confessed all the sins she knew to confess, but still experienced feelings of guilt.

One quiet evening, she sat at her desk with a Bible and concordance. She was determined to find out God's attitude toward the failures and faults of His children. At the top of the page, she wrote, *What God Does with Our Sins.* Then, she listed seventeen truths she discovered in the Scriptures, in this order:

- He lays them on His Son—Jesus Christ (Isa. 53:6).
- Jesus Christ takes them away (John 1:29).
- They are removed as far as the east is from the west (Ps. 103:12).
- When sought for, they are not found (Jer. 50:20).
- The Lord forgives them (Eph. 1:7).
- He cleanses them all away by the blood of His Son (1 John 1:7).
- He cleanses them as white as snow or wool (Isa. 1:18; Ps. 51:7).
- He abundantly pardons them (Isa. 55:7).
- He remembers them no more (Heb. 10:17).
- He casts them behind His back (Isa. 38:17).
- He casts them into the depths of the sea (Mic. 7:19).
- He will not impute us with sins (Rom. 4:8).
- He covers them (Rom. 4:7).
- He blots them out (Isa. 43:25).
- He blots them out as a thick cloud (Isa. 44:22).
- He blots out even the proof against us, nailing it to His Son's cross (Col. 2:14).[6]

The reality of what God had done with her sins delivered Rosalind from the guilt she had felt. Without so much access to Scripture,

David came to the same conclusions. As we imitate the principles found in his prayer of confession, we'll find the same forgiveness, cleansing, and joy. Praise God! His mercy takes away our guilt.

SUGGESTED SCRIPTURE

Psalm 103:1–12

PRAYER GUIDE

Praise God . . .

- for His Word.
- for His holiness.
- for all His blessings.
- for forgiving all your sins.
- for His love, grace, and mercy.
- for His righteousness and justice.
- for not giving the death that sin deserves.
- for removing your sin as far as east is from the west.

Day 20

HOW TO MAKE FAILURE FAIL

> For this cause everyone who is godly
> shall pray to You in a time when You
> may be found. . . . (Ps. 32:6)

> The reason why many fail in battle
> is because they wait until the hour
> of battle. The reason why others
> succeed is because they have gained
> their victory on their knees long
> before the battle came. Anticipate
> your battles; fight them on your
> knees before temptation comes,
> and you will always have victory.
> —R. A. Torrey[1]

Prayer can prevent failure.

"Do you think he was having a daily quiet time?"

Several years ago, a close friend asked that question about another friend. We had just watched the guy self-destruct. His anger had become explosive. His language toward his wife, children, and coworkers had turned abusive. He was making one rash decision after another. His moral compromises ultimately would cause him to walk away from his marriage and family.

The question echoed: Was our friend having a daily quiet time? The obvious answer seemed to be no. That question brought another to mind: Could this man have prevented the personal meltdown that had devastated his wife, his children, his parents, his friends, and his church simply by spending time daily with God in prayer and Bible study?

Yes, he could have.

It is not that people who pray and read the Bible every day are immune to sin. Almost every Christian has experienced the frustration of having a wonderful devotional time, then saying or doing something hours—or even minutes—later that was regretted.

However, when we are seeking God on a consistent basis, He will keep us from patterns of spiritual failure. God tells us that He is able to keep us from stumbling, and to present us faultless before the presence of His glory (Jude 24). When we are walking with God daily through prayer and Bible study, He will guard us from going astray. When we do disobey God, He will convict us to confess our sins and receive His forgiveness (1 John 1:9). If we persist in our disobedience, He will correct us in love (Heb. 12:5–11). When we stay close, He will keep us clean.

We've already seen that David's spiritual breakdown did not appear out of a clear blue sky. The storm was brewing long before the lightning struck. David had allowed his spiritual life to slip away from where it needed to be, so he had become vulnerable to temptation and sin. In Psalm 32, the Holy Spirit uses David's words to warn us not to risk spiritual failure by neglecting intimacy with God.

EVERYONE WHO IS GODLY SHALL PRAY

"For this cause," David says, "everyone who is godly shall pray to You in a time when You may be found" (Ps. 32:6). Let's take a moment to consider the ideas here.

David talks about the motivation for our prayers. When he says, "for this cause," David is pointing back to the things he had been talking about in the psalm. He urges us to cry out to the Lord in prayer because God forgives transgression, covers sin, removes iniquity, and cleanses deceit (Ps. 32:1–2). He urges us to cry out because keeping silent about sin makes us miserable, physically and emotionally (vv. 3–4); and because God's forgiveness comes only when we acknowledge and confess our sin (v. 5). God's gracious and merciful nature draws us to prayer.

Based on this motivation, David says "everyone who is godly shall pray." The word *godly* translates a Hebrew term that is very close in form to the word for God's loving-kindness, or faithful love (e.g., Ps. 51:1). A godly person is someone who has personal experience with the unfailing love of God and who reflects the same faithfulness and love back to God. This is the type of person who will pray.

People who do not have a relationship with God, on the other hand, will not cry out to Him. Even when they are paying a high price for their sin, the ungodly refuse to call on His name. When unsaved people are convicted of sin, they become angry with themselves, with others, or with God. They become bitter and resentful. They make excuses or simply harden themselves to the pangs of guilt. What they *won't* do, however, is pray. Instead, ungodly people will carry on with their sin.

One way of testing whether you have a saving relationship with Christ is to ask: "What do I do when I sin?" If you sin without feeling the need to seek God's forgiveness, you probably don't know God personally.

Rather than continuing in sin, David writes that "everyone who is godly shall pray to [God] in a time when [He] may be found." Do you hear the urgency in those words? God has promised us forgiveness, but He has not promised us tomorrow. If there is a time that God may be found, logic tells us that a time will come when He may not be found. The time to go to Him in prayer is always *now*, while His Spirit is still convicting us, while our conscience is still sensitive to our sin, and while we have the opportunity.

God says that when we have a relationship with Him, we will pray. We will seek and cherish closeness to Him. As we pray, God promises to accomplish a number of things in our lives. He will preserve us. He will guide us. And He will surround us with His mercy and forgiveness.

THROUGH PRAYER, GOD WILL PRESERVE YOU

A man is sitting on his rooftop—which now looks more like an island, because it's surrounded by water. The flood has left him stranded there for days. He's hungry, he's thirsty, and he wonders if he's going to make it out alive. Then he hears the *chop-chop-chop-chop-chop* of an approaching helicopter's rotors.

He stands up and turns in every direction. He can see the helicopter coming toward him. Though weakened by lack of food and dehydration, he jumps up and down on the roof, waving a white towel over his head with all the energy he can muster. The Coast Guard officers see the man. They hover over his house, lower a rescue basket down to him, and lift him up to safety.

In late August 2005 in the United States, that sort of scene was all too common along the coast off the Gulf of Mexico after Hurricane Katrina made landfall in Mississippi and Louisiana and flooded much of New Orleans. People were crying out, hoping to be rescued. In the same way, God reaches down to us with deliverance when we call on Him. He preserves us through our prayers. "Surely in a flood of great waters they shall not come near him. You are my hiding place; You shall preserve me from trouble; You shall surround me with songs of deliverance" (Ps. 32:6b–7).

David pictures the distress of sin as a heavy downpour during a storm. As a shepherd, David had watched violent storms come out of nowhere to turn dry, shallow valleys called wadis into raging torrents. A normally safe feeding place could suddenly be perilous for shepherd and sheep. Experienced shepherds knew when to search for a place of refuge, a hiding place.

Perhaps David had on occasion found protection from a storm

under a rocky cliff or in a cave. Facing the storm of his sin, David knew that he needed the shelter that only God's hand could provide. David testified that God preserved him from trouble. Through confession and repentance, he was able to sing of God's powerful deliverance from sin's guilt and destruction.

God, our hiding place and shelter, will deliver us and preserve our lives when we call on Him.

THROUGH PRAYER, GOD WILL GUIDE YOU

Not only does God deliver us from sin; He also offers counsel about the path ahead. In Psalm 32:8, the perspective of the psalm changes. It is no longer David talking about the Lord. Now the Lord speaks to David, saying, "I will instruct you and teach you in the way you should go; I will guide you with My eye." God promises to guide us in three ways when we seek Him in prayer.

He will instruct us. God's wisdom is the practical guidance we need in order to please Him. God assures us that if we ask Him for wisdom, He will give it to us (James 1:5).

He will teach us. The Hebrew word for "teach" also can mean to shoot an arrow. When God teaches us, He does much more than merely put information into our heads; He actually aims us like an archer aims an arrow. By His strength, He empowers us to go in the right direction.

He will guide us with His eye. God shows His love by promising to keep us on track, not with a heavy rod but with His eye. Think about the importance of the eyes in the relationship between a parent and a child. A caring mother will always keep an eye on her child. She's watching to see where her child is, what the child is doing, and what dangers are about. A wise child also learns to watch her mother's eyes, because her eyes signal whether she's relaxed or concerned. As children of God, Christians must constantly stay under the Father's watchful eye. We must look to Him and live to please Him.

God warns us against rejecting His guidance, saying, "Do not be like the horse or like the mule, which have no understanding, which must be harnessed with bit and bridle, else they will not come near you" (Ps. 32:9). A horse tends to go in any direction its feet happen to take it if there is no command. A mule tends to be stubborn, and to lag behind. Both horses and mules must be forced to obey by wearing a bridle. God tells us not to be like either of those animals. On the contrary, we should become sensitive to the Lord's leading, so that He does not need the harsher disciplines of life to bring us into line.

God wants us to respond willingly and joyfully to His guidance. He doesn't want us to come to Him in prayer because we're forced to by our circumstances, but because we're drawn to Him by love.

THROUGH PRAYER, GOD WILL SURROUND YOU

In the last verses of Psalm 32, the perspective turns back to David. He offers a study in contrasts: "Many sorrows shall be to the wicked; but he who trusts in the LORD, mercy shall surround him. Be glad in the LORD and rejoice, you righteous; and shout for joy, all you upright in heart!" (vv. 10–11).

David says the wicked will experience many sorrows as a result of their sin. His language indicates that those who continue in sin will suffer torment and increasing trouble because they are not seeking God. The apostle Paul sounded a similar warning to people with hardened and unrepentant hearts, saying they were storing up God's anger "in the day of wrath and revelation of the righteous judgment of God, 'who will render to each one according to his deeds'" (Rom. 2:5–6).

What has sin ever done for you? Someone might answer, "Sin has made me rich" or "Sin has given me enjoyment." The Bible acknowledges that sin offers "passing pleasures" (Heb. 11:25). But, in the end, sin offers nothing but sorrow.

A beer company billboard that appeared near our home several years ago showed a man out on a speedboat, a beautiful woman at his side and a beer in his hand. The sign read, "It just doesn't get any better than this."

The sign was true. Sin *doesn't* get any better than that. It will get a whole lot worse, but no better. An alcohol advertisement would never show a drunken man facedown in a gutter somewhere. It wouldn't show a wife being abused by her inebriated husband. It wouldn't show a car crash on the highway with whiskey and blood running together. It wouldn't show a little girl hiding under the bed in fear because her daddy had come home drunk. No, the Devil always manages to put sin in the most attractive package possible and say, "See, it doesn't get any better than this!"

What has sin done for you? After the short-lived pleasure and the fleeting thrill are over, what's left? Sin brings misery, bondage, regret, and sorrow. Even more importantly, sin brings God's anger and judgment, as well as a fracture in our fellowship with Him.

David had firsthand knowledge of the tragedy that comes to unrelenting sinners. As he covered up his sins, everything good in life evaporated. All that sin left him with was a residue of sorrow. But through God's forgiveness, David now found himself surrounded by God's unfailing love. "He who trusts in the LORD," David says, "mercy shall surround him." The Bible uses the same word translated "surround" to describe the children of Israel marching around the walled city of Jericho. They were surrounding that city so that God might bring it down. God surrounds us, however, that we might be lifted up. On every side and from all directions, He encompasses us with His faithfulness.

David concludes in Psalm 32:11 with three commands to those who have been forgiven by God:

- "Be glad in the LORD." He's not saying, "Put on a happy face." He's proclaiming that God's total forgiveness brings a down-to-the-bone delight that changes our entire disposition and outlook.
- "Rejoice." The Hebrew root word here means "to circle." The word picture that comes to mind is of a child spinning in circles out of joy.
- "Shout for joy." In the original language, this phrase is one word that indicates being overcome by God's joy.

Real joy in our lives is not something we can work up. It's something that God has to send down. In the quiet place of prayer—where God cleanses us of sin, delivers us from danger, and guides us in righteousness—a deep and inexplicable joy begins to wash over our souls.

WALKING WITH THE FATHER

A father and his teen daughter were close. They spent hours together each day in the late afternoon, walking around the neighborhood. Then the father began to notice a change. When he asked his daughter to go on a walk, she would make some excuse. He was sad that she wouldn't go walking with him. In every other way, things seemed the same. But each evening, he invited her to go walking, and then found himself strolling alone.

When his birthday came, the man's daughter presented him with a pair of exquisitely made bedroom slippers. They were beautiful. She told him, "Dad, I made these for you."

Now he knew what had been going on. She had been working on those slippers each night as he walked. "Sweetheart, I like these slippers very much," he said. "But next time, just let me have you all those days. I would rather have my child than anything you can make for me."

Don't overlook the importance of simply walking with your heavenly Father each day. Take it from David—a man who paid a steep price for neglecting his quiet time with God—nothing compares to what God will do in you as you delight in His presence through prayer.

SUGGESTED SCRIPTURE

Psalm 1

PRAYER GUIDE

As you spend time with your Father,

- pray that God will guide you while you walk with Him.
- ask for God's blessing on your life as you seek to please Him.
- praise God for His Word.
- delight in meditating on God's Word through the day.
- ask God to plant His Word deep in your heart.
- praise the Lord for guiding your steps as you follow His righteousness.

Day 21

EXPERIENCING GOD'S RENEWAL

The delicate, purple-pink blossoms of the fireweed make it one of the most beautiful wildflowers in Alaska.

Besides being pretty, fireweed blossoms have a number of uses. The flowers can be brewed as a tea to treat upset stomachs, coughs, and asthma. The blossoms can even be used in a flavorful jelly. The plant can be applied to treat bug bites, cuts, and eczema.

Fireweed gets its name because it is the first plant to bloom after a fire. When the smoke clears and the earth cools, these flowers emerge. Peeking through the ashes, fireweed covers the landscape like a stunning quilt, and turns the charred landscape into something beautiful once again.

So it is with God's forgiveness and renewal.

As David discovered, the effects of our sin can be more devastating than a wildfire, but God's grace makes our lives bloom again. Perhaps you have been brought low by spiritual or moral failure. Covering up the sin won't work. Ignoring guilt won't do any good. You feel helpless, and you are but for the grace of God.

God's grace and forgiveness are available through Jesus Christ. As you call on Him in prayer, you can begin anew. He is able to give those who come to Him "beauty for ashes, the oil of joy for mourning, the garment of praise for the spirit of heaviness; that they may be called trees of righteousness, the planting of the LORD, that He may be glorified" (Isa. 61:3).

SUGGESTED SCRIPTURE READING

Isaiah 61:1–3

PRAYER GUIDE

As you pray . . .

- thank God for sending Jesus to bring good news to the poor, healing to the brokenhearted, and liberty to the captives.
- praise God for His comfort during times of grief and sorrow.
- thank God for His faithfulness in forgiving sin and restoring sinners so that we can glorify Him.

Part 4

THE LORD'S PRAYER

Principles for Praying with Purpose

Prayer begins with worship.
Prayer clarifies our priorities.
Prayer requires unceasing trust.
Prayer brings God's protection.
Prayer magnifies God's character.

Day 22

TEACH ME TO PRAY, LORD

They could have asked Him to teach them . . .

- how to walk on water,
- how to calm the stormy seas,
- how to heal the sick,
- how to turn water into wine,
- or any of the other amazing things they had seen Jesus do.

Instead, the disciples begged Him, "Lord, teach us to pray" (Luke 11:1). They had watched Jesus long enough to understand that He knew how to talk to God. They desired the same intimacy and closeness to God that they observed in their Master's life.

In answer to their request, Jesus provided them a short but powerful model for praying. The Lord's Prayer appears two times in Scripture. In Luke 11, Jesus offered the prayer in response to the disciples' request. In Matthew 6, He taught this prayer as part of the Sermon on the Mount. Though the versions of the prayer in both gospels are nearly identical, the wording found in Matthew is the more familiar to most of us.

We will study the Lord's Prayer, phrase by phrase. Remember, Jesus did not give us this prayer to repeat mechanically. In fact, Jesus warns us not to pray with empty repetitions (Matt. 6:7). Instead, the Lord offered it as a model of complete prayer. He told His followers, "In this manner, therefore, pray" (v. 9). When we pray, Jesus want us to cover the same ground that He covered in this model prayer.

SUGGESTED SCRIPTURE READING

Luke 11:1–4; Matthew 6:9–13

PRAYER GUIDE

As you pray today,

- ask for Christ to continue teaching you to pray.
- ask for God to make each part of the Lord's Prayer real to you as you study it this week.
- ask God to help adjust your prayers to fit the model that Jesus has provided for His followers.

Day 23

Our Father's Holy Name

> Our Father in heaven, hallowed be
> Your name. (Matt. 6:9)
>
> It is right to call Him Holy; we
> speak truth when we call Him King.
> But if you want to touch His heart,
> use the name He loves to hear. Call
> Him Father.
>
> —Max Lucado[1]

Prayer begins with worship.

As a believer in Jesus Christ, you have a wonderful family relationship with God. When He looks at you, He sees His child. When you come to Him in prayer, you are coming to worship your Father.

A series of photos in *Life* magazine during the early 1960s showed the U.S. President John F. Kennedy sitting at his desk in the Oval Office. On the floor by his desk, his children, Caroline and John Jr., were playing with their toys. The images moved us because they showed that, although Kennedy was the president of the United States, he was also a father. He was the most powerful person in the world, but two small children were allowed to play at his feet because he was their daddy.

David Jeremiah saw an illustration of spiritual truth in those photos. He writes, "In the same way, God is both our Father and the Lord of glory. We can approach Him confidently in prayer because we are His dearly beloved children, but we must never forget that He is also the Sovereign of the universe."[2]

Jesus taught His disciples to start their prayers by worshipping God. The opening words of the Lord's Prayer—"Our Father in heaven, hallowed be Your name"—form the entrance way into God's presence. We enter His courts with praise, as the psalmist commanded (Ps. 100:4). Petitions will come later. Asking, requesting, and confession will have their place. But first, we worship God in prayer.

A TRANSFORMED RELATIONSHIP

To call God "Father," we must have a relationship with Him. Before we can address Him by that cherished name, we have to experience His salvation. Praying "our Father" as a true statement requires faith in Jesus Christ. Our trust in Jesus brings payment for our sins through His blood, forgiveness, and escape from sin's punishment. In addition to all of the other blessings of salvation, God says that faith in Jesus brings us into His family.

You have been adopted into God's household. The almighty Creator of the universe is your Father. "But when the fullness of the time had come, God sent forth His Son, born of a woman, born under the law, to redeem those who were under the law, that we might receive the adoption as sons. And because you are sons, God has sent forth the Spirit of His Son into your hearts, crying out, 'Abba, Father!'" (Gal. 4:4–6).

Through adoption, parents make an orphaned child a full member of the family. All of the privileges of being in the family—a home, a name, an inheritance, and a relationship with Mom and Dad—come when the adoptive parents sign the papers and take the child home.

That's exactly what God has done for us in Christ. He has brought us into His household, given us an eternal inheritance, promised us a new name, and extended to us the honor of calling Him our Father. The adoption He gives us is far greater than any human equivalent.

"We're having trouble with our adopted daughter," the man told me.

He began to talk about what was happening in his family. His teenaged girl was rebellious, getting in trouble at school and in the community, and causing her parents a lot of sorrow. Her problems were weighing on her dad's heart just as they would any father.

The man undoubtedly cared deeply for his daughter; it showed in every word he said. Except for one thing—the father referred to the girl more than once as his "adopted" daughter, even comparing her unfavorably to his older, "natural" son. Why would he keep making the point that his daughter was adopted? Perhaps that was just his manner of talking. Or perhaps he was subtly distancing himself from her. Each time he said "our adopted daughter," it was as though he was telling me, "She hasn't always been ours. She really belongs to another family."

God adopts us fully into His family. There are no qualifiers. There's no tag He puts on us to remind us that we once did not belong to Him. Through faith in Christ, we are His children, period. Though we were strangers from God and orphans in our sin, our relationship with Him transforms us eternally through Jesus Christ. We are in His family forever.

A TERM OF INTIMACY

Because we are His children, we can call Him "Father," a name that expresses closeness. Christ instructed us to pray, "Our Father." Behind the word *Father* is the Aramaic term *Abba*. *Abba* is an intimate word to use in speaking to God, a child's word that is the equivalent of "Daddy" or "Papa."

Abba was the term Jesus used in prayer. References to Jesus calling God "Father" occur more than two hundred times—156 times in the gospel of John alone! The first recorded words of Jesus in Scripture are, "Did you not know that I must be about My Father's business?" (Luke 2:49). The boy Jesus reminded His earthly parents that His deep and abiding relationship with God surpassed any earthly family bond. Then, at the end of His life, the Lord once again called on *"Abba"* as He breathed out the prayer, "Father, into Your hands I commit My spirit" (Luke 23:46).

We may not fully comprehend how remarkable it was for Jesus to address God as *Abba*. One New Testament scholar carefully examined the prayer literature of early Judaism. In all of ancient Jewish prayer literature, he found not one place where God is called *"Abba* Father." No Jew would have dared speak to God that way.[3] *Abba* was too cozy a word to use in talking to God. Yet Jesus used the word all the time.

The disciples had heard Jesus call God *Abba* throughout their time together with Him. "But that's just for Him," they must have thought, "not for us." You can imagine the looks of astonishment that must have filled their faces when they heard the Lord say, "When you pray, say *'Abba*.'" This was radical. As Jews, they had been taught not even to say God's name out loud for fear of dishonoring Him. Now, their Master was telling them to call God something so intimate, so informal as "Daddy"? It didn't make sense to the disciples.

But it made perfect sense to Jesus. He was going to make the way to bring them into God's family. He was empowering them to speak to God in the most familiar and trusting terms. What Jesus offered His disciples then, He offers all believers today. Because we are in Christ and Christ is in us, we can cry out to God as our Father and approach Him on the basis of a father-child relationship. Martin Luther once said that if he could just understand the first two words of the Lord's Prayer, he would never be the same again. Neither would we.

BREAKING FREE FROM EARTH'S SHACKLES

Erin came to her Bible study leader after class with tears streaming down her face.

"I really need to talk to you, Laura," she said.

They sat down in a back corner of the classroom as other members of the group left to go to the worship service. Erin began to share her story of a fractured family and an abusive, violent father.

"My dad hurt me in every way you can imagine," Erin said, "and when I hear the word 'father,' it's always his face that comes to my mind. How can I call God 'Father'? I know He would never treat me the way my dad did."

Erin is not alone. Other Christians find it hard to address God as "Father" because they grew up in homes with cruel, hurtful dads. Yet, God has revealed Himself to us as "Father," and He wants us to call Him by that name.

The need for emotional healing may be one of the reasons that Jesus instructs us to pray, "Our Father *in heaven*." He is vastly different from all the earthly fathers we have known here below. In Him, there is perfect love, unending forgiveness, boundless kindness, and unlimited grace. While "our Father" emphasizes God's closeness to us, "in heaven" expresses His majesty above us.

Jesus tells us to address God as "Our Father in heaven" because it becomes easy for us to imagine that God is like we are. We may begin to use the name "Father" cheaply, easily, and sentimentally. God *is* our Father, but He is *not* indulgent with His children. He does not shut His eyes to our sins, faults, and mistakes. Commentator William Barclay writes, "This God, whom we can call Father, is the God whom we must still approach with reverence and adoration, and awe and wonder."[4]

Wheaton College in Illinois once had a president named Raymond Edman. He was a missionary, an educator, an author, and a friend to countless people. Billy Graham once called him the most unforgettable Christian he ever met. Dr. Edman felt passionately about being reverent before God. He taught his students that coming to God in worship was a serious matter. One day as he was lecturing on worship, Edman began to tell about a time that he had visited with the emperor of Ethiopia. He described the preliminary briefings, the protocol he had to follow, and the way he bowed with respect as he entered the presence of the king.

"In the same way," he said, "we must prepare ourselves to meet God."

With those words, the college president slumped onto the pulpit and fell to the floor. Instantly, he had entered the presence of the King of Kings, his heavenly Father.[5]

Knowing that we worship our Father in heaven helps us to break free from the shackles of life here on earth. God has told us, "Heaven is My throne, and earth is My footstool" (Isa. 66:1). In heaven, our Father fully reveals His majesty and glory. In heaven, He displays His power and declares the fact that He is directing things from on high. The realization that He is our Father *in heaven* fills us with deep reverence as we pray.

REMEMBERING HIS HOLINESS

The call to worship that Jesus issues in the Lord's Prayer continues with a bold petition: "Our Father in heaven, hallowed be Your name." Do you see the progression of worship in the opening words of this prayer? We climb higher into God's exalted presence—from speaking intimately with our Father, to anticipating the glories of heaven, and then bowing before His overwhelming holiness. Charles Spurgeon made note of the increasing intensity in these words. He wrote, "The child lisping, 'Abba, Father,' grows into the cherub crying, 'Holy, Holy, Holy.'"[6]

"Hallowed be Your name." We don't use the word *hallowed* in ordinary speech. The word refers to something holy or sanctified. Holiness means purity and cleanness. But the word means more than that. At the heart of the concept of holiness is the idea of being set apart. Something holy is different from other things. For instance, the temple in Jerusalem was holy because it was set apart from all other buildings. The altar was holy because it was set apart for sacrifices. The Sabbath was different from all the other days of the week—set aside for rest and worship. God taught Israel to regard all of these things as holy in order to help His people understand His holiness. He is not like us. He is set apart. He is holy.

Jesus instructs us to pray, "Father, may Your name be made holy." In some ways, that request may seem strange to us. After all, how can God's name be made any holier than it already is? He is eternally and perfectly pure, clean, set apart, and sanctified. We can do nothing to make Him or His name more holy. Yet, we can ask for God to make us more aware of His holiness.

A visitor to an electrical plant was impressed by the number of warning signs he encountered. Again and again, he saw bright yellow signs reading, "High Voltage," "Do Not Touch," and "Danger!" The signs did not make the raw power being generated at the plant any more dangerous. But the warnings helped everyone there to remember what they were constantly working around.

In the same way, praying, "Hallowed be Your name," keeps us from forgetting the awesome majesty of our Father in heaven. We ask so that we will keep His name in the highest respect and honor. We pray that our lips might "give to the LORD the glory due His name" (Ps. 96:8).

WHAT'S HE WORTH TO YOU?

My wife and I were browsing in an antique store when a book sitting on a table caught my attention. The author was W. A. Criswell, the late preacher and pastor of the First Baptist Church of Dallas. The book was almost fifty years old, but in nearly immaculate condition. Inside the front cover, Dr. Criswell had autographed it. No Southern Baptist preacher in his right mind would leave that book lying there.

I took the volume to the sales desk. "There's no price on this book," the lady at the desk told me. "It's for display only." My heart sank a little.

Then she said, "I'll call the owner and see if he'd be willing to sell it."

We left our telephone number and continued shopping. The rest of the day, I wondered, "How much will the owner ask for it?" I determined that I'd pay no more than twenty or thirty dollars. Was the book worth even that much?

Two days later, the man who owned the book called. He asked me why I wanted the book. Then he replied, "Well, my family and I have visited your church. We appreciate what you folks are doing over there. If you'll pray for my family, I'll put a note on the book to let you have it as my gift. You can pick it up whenever you'd like."

I asked him about his family, promised to pray for them, and picked up the book a few days later. It has a prominent place on my desk. What I had been willing to pay for was given to me for free. Not only that, but because the man gave it as a gracious gift, that book is now worth far more than the dollar value I'd originally placed on it.

The meaning of the word *worship* closely relates to the idea of ascribing worth to something. Just how much is God worth? Every part of your relationship with Him has come without cost to you. The Father has freely given salvation through His Son. He has generously extended the honor of being in His family and of calling Him your Father. Our Father's giving nature requires a worshipful response.

SUGGESTED SCRIPTURE READING

1 Peter 1:3–21

PRAYER GUIDE

As you come before your holy, heavenly Father, you can worship Him because . . .

- He has brought you into His family.
- He has promised you an incorruptible inheritance.
- He provides you with joy that surpasses all your trials.
- He is holy, and has made the way for you to be holy.
- He has redeemed you with the precious blood of Jesus.

OUR FATHER'S COMING KINGDOM

Your kingdom come. Your will be
done on earth as it is in heaven.
(Matt. 6:10)

Lord, whatever you want, wherever
you want it, whenever you want it,
that's what I want.
—Clarence Macartney[1]

Prayer clarifies our priorities.

Recently I read a book on the life and work of Leonardo da Vinci.
It seems as though his brilliance was matched only by his ability to
become distracted. Time after time, he began great works that he left
incomplete.

In the middle of one painting that was bound to become another
masterpiece, Leonardo laid down his brushes and oils to answer a
knock at his door. A neighbor was having trouble with the waterline
at his house. He wondered if the great Leonardo—who seemed to
know something about everything—could take a look at it. The

artist picked up his tools and followed the distressed man home. The pipes may have been repaired, but the painting stands unfinished. The great artist let his priorities become confused.

God is never distracted from the work He is doing in us. Too often we let our priorities become confused, and we fail to fulfill the purpose to which God has called us.

KEEPING THINGS IN ORDER

God will use you in ways you could never even dream. That's one reason He has saved you through Jesus Christ. God says, "We are His workmanship, created in Christ Jesus for good works, which God prepared beforehand that we should walk in them" (Eph. 2:10). God makes your life His masterpiece as you align your priorities with His.

We can easily become sidetracked if we give high priority to the wrong things. Things that have little eternal significance are magnified. Our time and attention are occupied with matters that may not be important in God's eyes. In R. G. Lee's most well-known sermon, he bemoaned Christians with "incandescent light powers who make no more light for God than a smoky barn lantern," believers with "locomotive powers doing pushcart work for God," and people with "steam-shovel abilities who are doing teaspoon work for God."[2]

We are responsible to God for the way we order our lives. Prayer helps us to keep our values, our goals, and our daily schedules in line with God's purposes. After instructing His disciples to come into the Father's presence through worship, Jesus told them to bring this petition before the Father: "Your kingdom come. Your will be done on earth as it is in heaven" (Matt. 6:10). This request gets at the nuts and bolts of our lives. Jesus is telling us to follow God's lead as we order our goals and make our plans. Sometimes we may be planning in one direction when God's will is in another direction. Learning to pray first and plan afterward will change our personal priorities, our homes, our churches, and everything we do for Christ.

SEEKING GOD'S KINGDOM

"Your kingdom come." That request is filled with urgency. The Greek can be translated, "May Your kingdom come now!"

When Jesus told His followers to pray this way, He was reaffirming the main theme of His earthly ministry. You need only skim through the Gospels, and you will discover the dominance of God's kingdom in Christ's teaching. When Jesus first emerged on the scene in Galilee, He came preaching the good news of God's kingdom (Mark 1:14). He proclaimed the message of the kingdom as He traveled from city to city (Luke 8:1). God's kingdom consumed each sermon Jesus preached and each parable He told.

It's no wonder, then, that Jesus would teach us to pray, "Your kingdom come." He wants God's kingdom to be our top priority, just as it is His. This portion of the Lord's Prayer is similar to the command Jesus would give later in the Sermon on the Mount: "Seek first the kingdom of God and His righteousness, and all these things shall be added to you" (Matt. 6:33).

We are commanded to pursue God's kingdom with dogged determination. More than that, believers are to seek God's kingdom *first*, making His kingdom our magnificent obsession. When we pray, "Your kingdom come," we are saying, "God, may Your kingdom be the number-one goal of my life."

So, what does it mean to seek God's kingdom? What does it mean to pray for His kingdom to come?

God's kingdom does not consist of geographical territory or political power. Jesus was clear in saying that His kingdom is not of this world (John 18:36). Neither is God's kingdom primarily something that human beings can bring about on earth through our efforts to change society. Instead, to seek His kingdom and pray for His kingdom is to ask that Christ reign on the earth and in our lives.

John MacArthur has observed that praying for God's kingdom to come has three areas of application:

1. *The conversion of unbelievers.* The evangelistic element of this

prayer is that we are asking for God's kingdom to expand as more people trust Jesus Christ as Savior.

2. *The commitment of believers.* We are praying that God would take charge of our lives. As we submit to the lordship of Jesus Christ, God's kingdom comes to us as persons.

3. *The commencement of Christ's return.* Our prayer makes the same request that the apostle John made: "Come, Lord Jesus" (Rev. 22:20). We are asking for the day to come when Jesus descends and establishes His kingdom on earth.[3]

NOTHING COULD BE BETTER

After the petition "Your kingdom come," Jesus instructs us to pray, "Your will be done." Asking for God's will to be done is an intensely personal request. Christ's intention is that we pray with trust that His will is the absolute best for our lives. Even if God's will causes us to suffer or those around us to grieve, nothing could be better than His will.

In January 1956, U.S. missionaries Jim Elliot, Pete Fleming, Ed Mc-Cully, Nate Saint, and Roger Youderian were attempting to make first contact with the Huaorani Indians of Ecuador, often referred to as Aucas. On the morning of January 8, Nate Saint—the team's pilot—failed to make a promised radio contact. The next day another pilot flew out to the Curaray River, home of the Huaorani, and saw Saint's small plane on the beach, stripped of its fabric. The U.S. Air Rescue Service in Panama received a call for help and the search began.

The story spread. People around the globe were listening to the accounts of the rescue party's search until the bodies were discovered on a sandbar by the river. The Huaorani had speared the missionaries to death. The January 28, 1956, issue of *Life* Magazine published an account of the missionaries' attempts to reach these remote people. Water-stained film recovered from a camera found in the river showed smiling missionaries visiting with the villagers who would massacre them. The pictures were published alongside photos of the grieving widows and nine fatherless children.

At the time, the story was heartbreaking, but we now know that the radical commitment and personal sacrifice of these martyrs later reaped wonderful results. Many Huaorani came to know Christ, led to faith in Jesus by the widows of the men they had killed. Many Christian young people responded to the call to service after hearing of the five martyrs and their families. God turned tragedy into triumph.

Of the five slain missionaries, Elliot has become the best known through the books written by his widow, Elisabeth. Through these books, his words and example inspired a generation of Christians to go to the mission field or to live more mature and sacrificial Christian lives in other ways. Many caught the vision of the motto Elliot adopted at age twenty: "He is no fool who gives what he cannot keep to gain what he cannot lose."[4]

In one of his journal entries, Elliot made another declaration concerning God's will in his life. The words speak powerfully in light of the place where God's will took Jim Elliot: "I have found that the most extravagant dreams of boyhood have not surpassed the great experience of being in the will of God, and I believe that nothing could be better."[5]

Think about those last four words: *Nothing could be better.* We will never truly pray, "Your will be done" until we know that nothing is better for us than to be in God's will.

So the attitude with which we pray "Your will be done" is crucial. We can say it with a voice of defeat. Like a scrawny kid who tries without success to arm wrestle a body builder, we can drop our heads and sigh in exhaustion, "I give up, Lord. You're too strong for me. I can't fight with You and win." We can say, "Your will be done" with resentment. When Eli the priest learned that God was going to strip the priesthood from his family because of his sons' wickedness, he said, "It is the LORD. Let Him do what seems good to Him" (1 Sam. 3:18). He accepted God's will, but there may have been a hint of bitterness in his tone. A calloused heart says, "I don't like Your will, Lord, but I can't do anything about it."

God's plan, however, is that we would say, "Your will be done" with an attitude of love and trust. The surrendered heart prays, "God, I know that Your will is the absolute best for me. God, I know that You love me completely. So, Lord, let Your will happen in my life." When we trust in the love of God, it becomes easier to say, "Your will be done."

Praying for God's will in your life requires . . .

- *emptying yourself of your own will.* If you are holding on to your own wishes, you are not ready to hear and do the Father's will.
- *committing to stay close daily.* Knowing and following God is a step-by-step process that affects our individual decisions. You must stay close to Him daily because He guides continually and His will requires daily surrender.
- *promising to obey.* Nothing could be better than to seek and obey His will, no matter what the cost.

As we pray every day according to God's will, the Father synchronizes our lives with His priorities.

A SLICE OF HEAVEN ON EARTH

Matthew 6:10 says that God's will is to be done "on earth as it is in heaven." Jesus instructs us to pray that God's will is accomplished to the same utter completion that it occurs among the angels of heaven. Think about the truths implied by this final phrase.

First, God's will is not always done on earth. Some people—even some Christians—mistakenly think of God's will in the same way that the ancient Greeks thought of fate. They believe that whatever happens is destined to happen. It's all set in stone, so there's no real need to pray. *Not true*, says Jesus. God in His providence has chosen to accomplish His will through our prayers.

Second, believers are able to do God's will on earth, just as it is done in heaven. How is God's will done in heaven?

Joyfully, constantly, completely, and immediately.

When God reveals His will to the angels, they don't say, "Lord, we promise to do that, first thing tomorrow." Instead, they obey Him instantly. David Jeremiah writes, "The angels do the will of God . . . because they have just been commanded by the greatest Power in the universe, a Power they would never defy. When He commands, they obey."[6] A heart yielded to God in prayer is empowered to obey God.

When we become so sold out to God's priorities that we do His will on earth as it is done in heaven, our lives will become slices of heaven on earth, our homes will resonate with celestial joy, and our churches will seem like colonies of the New Jerusalem. That's exactly the way God intends for it to be. He desires for us to do His will the same way it is done in His courts above.

He wants our priorities to be heavenly priorities.

A BRAND-NEW SONG

For country music artist Ricky Skaggs, 1996 was an extremely difficult year. His father was dying with cancer, his mentor—bluegrass music legend Bill Monroe—died, and Ricky found himself wondering how to follow God's plan for his life.

Skaggs had first shared the platform with Monroe when Ricky was only six years old. Having heard about the boy mandolin picker, Monroe called him to the stage, handed him his own mandolin, adjusted the strap to fit Ricky's shoulder, and said, "Okay, son, let's hear some music." From that moment on, Skaggs knew that God wanted him to play bluegrass.

In the early 1980s, he moved to Nashville with his sights set on a record deal. Music agents told him that, while bluegrass was great, he needed to play mainstream country music to sell a lot of records. He took their advice and began to have success. Every now and then, though, Monroe or his dad would ask, "Ricky, when are you going to make a bluegrass album?" He would always give the same answer, "When the time is right, I will."

In the mid 1990s, Monroe's heart started to fail. When Skaggs visited him in the nursing home, Monroe would reach for the mandolin that sat by his bed next to his Bible and play a tune. Then he'd hand the instrument to Ricky, who would pick a tune himself. During one visit, Skaggs saw that the old man's heart problems had gotten much worse. At a loss for what to say, he took the mandolin, played a few licks, and then held it out to Monroe. The man known as "the Father of Bluegrass" shook his head. The sparkle in his eyes had disappeared. Bill Monroe died a few weeks later.[7]

Heartbroken at having lost his hero, Skaggs stood at a crossroads. Would he continue down the road that had brought him wealth and fame, or would he risk doing something different? He sensed the Lord was saying to him, "I want you to be where hurting people are, to be where people need to hear of My love."

Surrendering his priorities to God, he cut his band to eight musicians, started his own record company, and began appearing at festivals, churches, hospitals, county fairs, and even casinos, playing bluegrass music and proclaiming the gospel of Jesus Christ. His bluegrass sound draws unbelievers, but when they hear Ricky Skaggs, they hear the gospel. Thousands have been touched for Christ through a man who adjusted his life to God's plan.

"In the beginning, the enemy was in my ear: 'What happens if this doesn't work out? You won't be able to make a real living doing this,'" Skaggs says. "But God kept saying, 'Trust Me.'"[8]

God may be saying the same thing to you today. He has a plan for you that requires a realignment of your priorities. His purpose for your life requires seeking His kingdom and obeying His will. He will conform your will to His as you pray. Trust Him.

SUGGESTED SCRIPTURE READING

Psalm 40:5–8

PRAYER GUIDE

As you seek God in prayer,

- ask the Father to open your ears so that you can follow His will daily.
- ask God to help you obey His will and lay down your own wishes.
- delight in God, praising Him for His will for your life.

Day 25

OUR FATHER'S CONSTANT CARE

Give us this day our daily bread.
And forgive us our debts, as we forgive our debtors. (Matt. 6:11–12)

A man can no more take in a supply
of grace for the future than he can
eat enough for the next six months,
or take sufficient air into his lungs
at one time to sustain life for a week.
We must draw upon God's boundless store of grace from day to day
as we need it.

—D. L. Moody[1]

Prayer requires unceasing trust.

My father is a barber, but not at some small-town hang-around-
all-Saturday-morning-and-chew-the-fat barbershop. Dad's shop is
one of the busiest places you'll ever visit, with clippers buzzing and
scissors snipping all day long. Only two things stop my dad and the

other barbers from cutting hair, and that's when the phone rings or when someone new walks into the shop. There's ordinarily just one reason that someone calls or walks in—to ask for a haircut.

For me it is different. After years as a pastor and seminary professor, lots of people call me on the phone or come into my office to talk about all kinds of things. Some ask for counsel about personal details of their lives. But no one has ever asked the question my father hears each day: "Can I have a haircut?"

That's just as well, since I don't know how to give a haircut. So, even if someone who visited needed a haircut, he wouldn't ask me for one, knowing that I can't meet that particular need.

You will not come to God with the deepest needs of your heart unless you are convinced that He can do something to meet those needs. Willow Creek Community Church pastor, Bill Hybels, is transparent about his own struggles with this fact. "In my head I have always believed in God's omnipotence," he writes, "but too often this belief hasn't registered where it really counts—in my heart. When my heart is not persuaded, I don't pray about difficult situations and ask God to fulfill pressing needs. Somewhere, deep down, I don't believe he can do anything about them."[2]

Trusting in God's power to answer motivates us to pray. Doubt about His power keeps us from praying.

A DAY-BY-DAY TRUST

Jesus taught His disciples to pray in total trust and dependency on God. In His next words in the Lord's Prayer, "Give us this day our daily bread," Jesus used grocery store language to express a day-by-day reliance on God's care. He teaches us to ask the Father, "Give us the bread we need for the coming day. Give us the things we need to eat when the children come home from school and the family gathers around the table." Jesus wants us to pray with down-to-earth trust in our Father.

The request, "Forgive us our debts, as we forgive our debtors," calls for day-by-day prayer as well. With each day, we commit sins for which we need to be forgiven. We also will have occasion to forgive others on a daily basis. By instructing His disciples to seek and grant forgiveness, Jesus was calling for them to depend on God constantly.

One New Year's Day, a little girl wrote a letter as her younger brother looked on. Her letter read:

> To Whom It May Concern,
>
> I would like to place an order for 365 good days. Your swift response would be appreciated.
>
> Sincerely,
> Sarah Jane Smith

After signing the letter, Sarah Jane told her brother matter-of-factly, "If you want good days, it's best to order them a year at a time."

We are not wise to pray a year at a time, or even a week at a time. Long-range planning is smart, but long-range praying is nearly impossible. So, Jesus tells us to pray day by day. God has designed our lives to move one day at a time. His Word says, "You do not know what will happen tomorrow. For what is your life? It is even a vapor that appears for a little time and then vanishes away" (James 4:14).

We don't know what tomorrow has in store, so we trust God for today. We get through sickness one day at a time. We struggle through financial pressure one day at a time. We deal with crises in our families one day at a time. To meet our daily challenges with the power, grace, and peace of God, we must pray and trust Him daily.

ENOUGH FOR TODAY

"Give us this day our daily bread." This request would have resonated in the hearts of the Lord's disciples. As Jews, they knew how God rained down manna each day for the children of Israel to eat as they journeyed through the wilderness. God provided detailed instructions about collecting the manna. Israelites were forbidden to gather more than a one-day supply. Only on the day before Sabbath could they get enough for an extra day. Otherwise, if they tried to store up manna, the bread would spoil. God was teaching them to trust Him to provide day by day.

Correspondingly, Jesus told His followers to request bread for the day. We can compare praying for daily bread to asking God for the necessities that sustain our lives. Asking the Lord to "give us this day our daily bread" can include praying for Him to supply our food, to sustain our health, to bring us favorable weather conditions, to watch over our safety, and to provide anything else that pertains to our welfare each day.

Praying for daily bread accomplishes several things:

It reminds us that God is the source of all provision. "Every good gift and every perfect gift is from above, and comes down from the Father of lights, with whom there is no variation or shadow of turning" (James 1:17). He is the one who provides.

A seven-year-old boy asked his father why they thanked God before eating. The father picked up a dinner roll and said, "Where does this come from?"

The boy answered, "From the grocery store."

"But who made it?" the father asked.

"The bakery, I guess."

"But where did the baker get the flour to make it?"

"From the farmer," his son said.

"Right," said the father. "And how did the farmer grow his crop?"

"He planted a seed."

Now, Dad was in scoring position. He asked, "And who made the seed?"

"God did!" his boy exclaimed.

"That," his father answered, "is why we thank Him."

Asking God to take care of us each day keeps us from forgetting that—while we work and make the effort to provide for our needs—He is the ultimate source of all that we have. We are depending on Him.

Praying for our daily bread reminds us that God satisfies our needs, not our every wish. God has promised to supply the needs of those who trust Him. David gave this testimony of God's provision: "I have been young, and now am old; yet I have not seen the righteous forsaken, nor his descendants begging bread" (Ps. 37:25).

Jesus used the example of bread when He talked about praying for God's provision. Bread is the most basic of foods; it contains the essentials to sustain us. Jesus does not instruct us to pray, "Give us this day our daily prime rib," or "Give us this day our daily chocolate cake." Instead, Jesus told us to ask God to meet our basic needs. Rather than praying, "Father, give me everything I want," the Lord teaches us to pray, "Father, give me what I need today."

God will give us what we need as we ask Him. He does not promise to make every Christian wealthy. Neither is He obligated to make us healthy. But God does promise to take care of us. He wants us to trust Him enough to be content with the blessings He chooses to send.

Praying for our daily bread reminds us we are not alone in our needs. Notice the pronouns in the petition: "Give *us* this day *our* daily bread." Jesus told His disciples to pray not only for their own needs but also the needs of others.

There's a traditional Canadian mealtime prayer that expresses the same type of selflessness Jesus was teaching. The prayer goes this way:

> For food in a world where many walk in hunger;
> For faith in a world where many walk in fear;
> For friends in a world where many walk alone;
> We give you humble thanks, O Lord.[3]

When we pray for our needs, Jesus does not want us to forget others who are needy. Instead, we are to pray that as God blesses us, He will also bless those around us.

OUR NEED TO BE FORGIVEN

The needs we bring to God are not only physical; our deeper needs are spiritual. Jesus teaches us to pray, "Forgive us our debts." With those words, Jesus instructs us to seek God's forgiveness for sin. Before the Father in prayer, we are aware of our constant need for cleansing and forgiveness.

In the Greek New Testament, five different words refer to *sin*. Each reveals a different dimension of spiritual need.

- *Hamartia* most frequently occurs. It was used of military bowmen missing a target. Sin falls short of what we could have been.
- *Parabasis* is usually translated "transgression." The word literally speaks of stepping across a line. We enter territory where God says not to go.
- *Paraptōma* can be called a trespass or an offense. It means to slip or blunder. Though this type of sin may not be as deliberate as *parabasis*, the result is the same.
- *Anomia* means lawlessness. It is the sin of knowingly breaking God's law.
- *Opheilēma*—the word Jesus used in the Lord's Prayer—occurs only a few times in the New Testament. It refers to a moral debt or a spiritual failure.

Each day we say things, think things, and do things that displease God. We neglect to do what He wants us to do. Because of this reality, Jesus tells us that our prayers should include asking the Father to forgive the debt of sin that we accumulate each day. Prayer and confession keep our hearts clean in the sight of God.

In that upper room in Jerusalem on the evening before Christ's crucifixion can be found a moving illustration of spiritual cleansing. Jesus took a basin of water and began to wash His disciples' feet. It was a house slave's task, but the Master went to each man and cleaned the grime and filth off the soles of their feet.

Simon Peter balked. "You'll never wash my feet!" he protested.

Jesus said, "If I don't wash your feet, you have no part of Me."

Peter exclaimed, "Then wash my hands and my head too!"

Do you remember how Jesus answered? He said, "He who is bathed needs only to wash his feet, but is completely clean" (John 13:10a).

In the Lord's words, we see a picture of our need for God's continual forgiveness. Dirt on the feet stands for the daily contamination we experience from sin. Believers need continual confession and cleansing of sin because every day we fall short of God's perfect holiness. Through prayer, we come to our Father and say, "Lord, my feet have gotten dirty again; I need You to wash them."

SENDING IT AWAY

Jesus addresses another need in this petition—the need to forgive others. Jesus tells us to pray, "Forgive us our debts as we forgive our debtors." Just as much as we need God's physical provision and just as deeply as we require His forgiveness, we also need to forgive others who sin against us. Later, Jesus told His disciples, "If you forgive men their trespasses, your heavenly Father will also forgive you. But if you do not forgive men their trespasses, neither will your Father forgive your trespasses" (Matt. 6:14–15). An unforgiving heart is a place of danger.

A man's wife had wounded him deeply. Though he had pretended to forgive, he felt a lingering bitterness toward her. Each time he felt that secret loathing, an angel came to the man and dropped a small pebble—barely the size of a shirt button—into his heart. Every time a pebble dropped, the man would feel a stab of pain. With each day, the pebbles multiplied. The man's heart grew so heavy that the top half of his body bent forward. He had to strain his neck upward in order to see straight ahead.[4]

When we refuse to forgive, our hearts become weighed down and our prayers are hindered. That's why we are to pray, "Forgive us our debts, as we forgive our debtors." To pray that is to say, "Father, forgive me in the same measure I've forgiven other people." The verb *aphiēmi*, translated "forgive," means "to send away." That's what God does when He forgives. He sends away our sins and offenses. They are gone. He commands us to do the same. When you come before God in prayer, you have a real need to send away the things done against you. You need to forgive your spouse, your friend, your parents, your child, your boss, your coworker, your fellow church member, or someone else who has hurt you.

MORE THAN SUFFICIENT

A hiker carried a small canteen. The way he rushed toward a stream of water revealed how thirsty he was. Yesterday, he had been able to eat and drink all he needed. Today he had filled his canteen before starting out, but after hours of hiking mountain trails, the canteen was dry, and he felt dehydrated and weary. When he came upon a rippling stream, he hurried to its bank, dipped his cup, and drew out water. As the cool water dripped down his chin, he reached down for another cupful. The stream supplied all the water he needed.

So it is when we come to the Father with our needs. Whether our need is for daily strength and sustenance, cleansing from sin, or grace to forgive, He is more than sufficient. Day by day, we can place our trust in Him.

SUGGESTED SCRIPTURE READING

Psalm 86:1–6

PRAYER GUIDE

As you pray,

- ask God to provide for your daily needs.

- ask God to forgive each sin you have committed.
- ask God to give you the merciful spirit to forgive others.
- praise God for His goodness, forgiveness, and grace.

Day 26

OUR FATHER'S
DELIVERING POWER

And do not lead us into temptation,
but deliver us from the evil one.
(Matt. 6:13a)

A ship in harbor is safe—but that is
not what ships are built for.
                          —John A. Shedd[1]

Prayer brings God's protection.

Some things that appear hazardous are less dangerous than the safer-looking alternatives. The chance of dying in a commercial airline crash is one in eight hundred thousand. One in five thousand die in an auto crash. Though your stomach may tighten as you take off in an airplane, riding on tons of metal thrust through the air by huge jet engines still is safer than being pulled along in a six-cylinder machine that never leaves the ground.[2]

God has not called believers to a risk-free life. We live on a battle-field, not a playground. In a life of temptations, dangers, and trials, even the places that look safest hide spiritual perils.

Jesus does not command us to pray to be removed from the battlefield but to be protected as we fight. Two petitions in the Lord's Prayer capture the idea of battlefront praying. He instructed His disciples to ask the Father, "Do not lead us into temptation, but deliver us from the evil one" (Matt. 6:13a).

SOME SERIOUS QUESTIONS

Jesus tells us to pray, "Lead us not into temptation." Those words—like all the words of this prayer—are probably familiar. But this request may be the hardest in the prayer to understand and apply. The words of this request bring up important questions.

One question is how a holy, righteous God leads anyone to be tempted. Jesus's words would be easier to comprehend if He had told us to pray, "Father, don't allow Satan to lead me into temptation," or "Father, don't let the world lead me into temptation," or "Father, keep my own flesh from leading me into temptation." We know that the Devil wants us to sin, that the world tries to influence us, and that our flesh desires things contrary to God's Spirit.

But Jesus doesn't mention the world, the flesh, or the Devil here. Instead, He tells us to pray, "God, don't lead us into temptation." Would God ever desire anyone to be enticed by sin? Would He dangle temptation like the juicy bait on a rusty hook that lures an unsuspecting fish? *Absolutely not!* God tells us, "Let no one say when he is tempted, 'I am tempted by God'; for God cannot be tempted by evil, nor does He Himself tempt anyone" (James 1:13). God is so pure, so perfect, and so good that He would never try to persuade you to sin. When Jesus tells us to pray, "Lead us not into temptation," He clearly isn't telling us that God will lead us into sin if we neglect to ask Him not to do so. Something more is communicated in His words that may not be immediately visible.

So what does the Bible mean by temptation? Perhaps what is needed is a better understanding of temptation. In English, temptation is negative, carrying the idea of being seduced. The Greek word—*peirasmos*—is more neutral. While it can be used of temptation to sin, the word also can refer to a test of strength, loyalty, resolve, or ability. The word is translated "test" or "trial" elsewhere in Scripture.

Look, for example, at these uses of forms of *peirasmos*:

My brethren, count it all joy when you fall into various *trials*, knowing that the testing of your faith produces patience. (James 1:2–3)

Blessed is the man who endures *temptation*; for when he has been approved, he will receive the crown of life which the Lord has promised to those who love Him. (James 1:12)

Beloved, do not think it strange concerning the fiery *trial* which is to try you, as though some strange thing happened to you; but rejoice to the extent that you partake of Christ's sufferings, that when His glory is revealed, you may also be glad with exceeding joy. (1 Peter 4:12–13)

James and Peter are saying that, in these cases, trials and tests are causes for rejoicing. They strengthen faith and bring a reward. Significantly, the Bible also uses a form of *peirasmos* to describe the testing of Jesus by Jewish religious leaders. Luke 10:25 says, "A certain lawyer stood up and tested Him, saying, 'Teacher, what shall I do to inherit eternal life?'" The lawyer wasn't trying to tempt Jesus to sin. Instead, he was putting pressure on Jesus to give him an answer. Each time Jesus was tested in this way, He turned the test into an opportunity to glorify God.

So, when Jesus told us to pray, "Lead us not into temptation," *temptation* is better understood as a test. As we pray for God to protect us from temptation, we are asking Him to keep us out of situations that severely test our vulnerability.

Understanding this truth, however, brings up another difficulty: *If tests produce blessings, rewards, and strength, why pray to escape them?* Testing can be good for Christians. We learn how to follow Christ more closely in times of pressure, and we gain greater wisdom and faith as a result.

So, why not pray *for* tests instead of praying to be delivered from them? A personal illustration from the classroom may help shed light on the reason. As a seminary professor, I scheduled tests every week. Students read their textbooks and memorized facts to be prepared for the weekly quizzes.

But, as their professor, I had the option of canceling any given quiz. At the start of the class, the students would be cramming last-minute facts into their heads, underlining passages in their books, studying their review sheets. Then I would stand at the lectern and ask, "Would anyone here be offended if I canceled this week's quiz?"

No one was ever offended.

Worried frowns turned into smiles, cheers might erupt, and I heard what a wonderful professor I was. Truth is, most of those students were ready for the test. Some would have earned high scores. But every student cheered when the quiz was canceled, because there was some possibility that even the best-prepared student might not do well on a particular exam.

Spiritual tests are much the same. Passing has rewards, but there's always a danger of failure. So Jesus tells us to pray, "Father, don't lead us into the place of testing when we don't have to be there."

Praying for God's protection means asking Him to keep us away from testing. In making this request, we can't forget the earlier petition, "Your will be done." Even as we ask God to lead us away from the tests, we are surrendering to God's will. Testing is part of God's plan for us. The Father allowed Job to be harshly tested and afflicted by Satan. The Holy Spirit even led Jesus into the wilderness for the purpose of being tempted by the Devil.

No one craves testing and temptation, but we know that times of trial are inevitable.

The application of praying, "Lead us not into temptation," becomes clearer when we consider it together with another portion of Scripture that deals with the same subject. The apostle Paul wrote,

"Let him who thinks he stands take heed lest he fall. No temptation has overtaken you except such as is common to man; but God is faithful, who will not allow you to be tempted beyond what you are able, but with the temptation will also make the way of escape, that you may be able to bear it" (1 Cor. 10:12–13).

Temptation in these verses can be interpreted as "testing," just as it is in the Lord's Prayer. Here, God's Word teaches us a number of things that are true about every test and temptation:

Every test can become a temptation to sin. The potential for failure exists any time we face a test. While testing can be a positive thing, we need to be aware that Satan turns tests into temptations. God allows tests to strengthen us, but our adversary, the Devil, subverts those tests into opportunities to pull us toward sin. That's why God warns, "Let him who thinks he stands take heed lest he fall." No Christian ever becomes immune to temptation.

Tests are somewhat predictable. When Paul wrote, "No temptation has overtaken you except such as is common to man," he was saying that God will not allow a brand-new test, never before experienced by any other human being, to come your way. Satan will not be able to brew up some fresh, unforeseen temptation to hurl. Instead, the tests, trials, and temptations we face have been encountered—and conquered—by other believers before us. By relying on God's Word and by the power of His Spirit, we can overcome every test.

Every test you face has been filtered through God's grace. In His grace, God makes certain that we are equipped to pass any test He allows to come our way.

God promises that He will not "allow you to be tempted beyond what you are able." God has already measured the difficulty levels on all the temptations you will ever face. None of them can defeat you unless you choose to let them. When the heat gets turned up in your life, you can be sure that God's hand is on the thermostat.

Every test you face has a way of escape. The Bible assures us that "with the temptation [God] will also make the way of escape." Tests and temptations that enter our lives have built-in escape hatches. Through faith in Christ, there's a way out. This causes our excuses to evaporate. We can't say, "The Devil made me do it," "I was just too weak," or "The temptation was much too strong." Many times God's way of escape comes through prayer to avoid tempting situations to begin with.[3]

Just a few months ago, my car's engine died while I was making a left-hand turn onto a busy road in rush hour traffic. No lights flashed on the dashboard announcing, "This is a test!" But it wasn't hard to discern that a trial of my patience and testimony had begun. It was the kind of trial that Christians face every day.

There was ample opportunity to sin in this little trial. It would be easy to lose patience over the stalled car or blow my temper with the other drivers who were honking their horns and giving mean looks and rude gestures. If I had sinned, Satan would have been successful in tempting me during that test. If, however, I came through this small trial with a Christlike spirit, then the test would become a tool in God's hand to make me a bit more mature in my faith. Thankfully, God's grace enabled me to pass the spiritual pop quiz. And a kind mechanic from a nearby garage got me back on the road.

When we pray for protection from temptation, we can ask,

- "Father, lead my steps far away from places that threaten me spiritually."
- "Give me strength and wisdom to avoid seeking those places for myself."
- "Place a watch over my eyes, my ears, my mouth, and my feet, that I might not sin."
- "Help me to see the escape You have provided for every temptation I face."

YOUR GREATEST ENEMY

In *The Screwtape Letters*, C. S. Lewis notes that people make two sorts of mistakes regarding the Devil and his demons. One is to disbelieve in the existence of these supernatural beings. The other is to think about them too much and have an unhealthy interest in them. The demons "are equally pleased by both errors."[4]

Jesus certainly believed in the reality of Satan. In the powerful intercessory prayer our Lord prayed for us, He asked the Father, "I do not pray that You should take them out of the world, but that You should keep them from the evil one" (John 17:15). And, in the second of the petitions we are considering in the chapter, He taught us to pray, "Deliver us from the evil one." Translations that simply render this, "Deliver us from evil," miss the thrust of what Jesus was saying. He was not merely talking about the presence of evil. He was thinking of the great enemy—Lucifer, the tempter, the Devil, Satan, the deceiver, the Prince of Darkness, the adversary—the Evil One.

Satan is real. We have already seen how he and demons can work to tempt us in times of testing. Through prayer, we ask God to deliver us from his wicked clutches. To be delivered from Satan means to be snatched from the terror of his attacks and the lure of his temptations. The word *deliver* refers to what we're delivered *from* but also what we're delivered *to*. Not only are we asking God to take us away from the evil schemes of the enemy, we are asking Him to draw us safely to Himself.

Take a moment to contemplate the delivering power of God. Our heavenly Father delivered . . .

- Israel from Egypt,
- Daniel from the lions' den,
- Esther from the evil Haman,
- David from the giant Goliath,
- Lot and his family from the city of Sodom,
- Rahab from the destruction of Jericho,
- Elijah from Jezebel and Ahab,
- Peter from drowning when he failed to walk upon the water, and
- Paul from all kinds of perils on land and sea.

The one God refused to deliver was His own Son. Instead, He surrendered Jesus to death for our transgressions so that we might be justified (Rom. 4:25). Through the sacrifice of Jesus on the cross, God defeated Satan fully, finally, and forever. In every imaginable situation, God has shown Himself strong and powerful to deliver His people from the assaults of the Evil One. When you face the Devil, our Father in heaven has the power to deliver you.

OUR ONLY SURE DEFENSE

On August 24, 2001, Michele steered the car into our driveway. It was about one o'clock, and she and our son Joshua were returning from the library. Michele pushed the button on the remote control to open the garage door, but nothing happened. She figured the battery on the remote had died, so she parked in the driveway and went into the house through the front door.

"Joshua, you go into the family room and look at your library book," she said. "I'm going to pull the car into the garage, and then I'll fix you some lunch."

When Michele opened the door between the house and the garage, she quickly noticed that three young men were in the back corner. They had broken into the house, turned off the power so that the garage door wouldn't open, and were gathering the things they had pilfered. She was startled but used her most authoritative voice to demand, "What are you doing?"

The men saw her, panicked, and ran out the door at the back of the garage. Michele slammed the kitchen door, grabbed Joshua and our dog, and ran out of the house in the other direction. Running past the kitchen window, she could see the men jumping over the fence in our backyard.

After she called the police from a neighbor's house, a patrol car arrived quickly. With guns drawn, police went through the house room by room to see if any intruders were still there. The robbers had gone, taking only a few things and doing minimal damage.

Later we thought about what *could* have happened. What if the men had ran toward Michele instead of away from her? What if someone had been waiting in the house? What if they had been armed? Each time we remember that day, we thank God for His protection and deliverance.

God has not called anyone to insulated safety. Christians stand on the front lines, facing spiritual and physical dangers and temptations. But He is able to deliver us as we call on Him in prayer. He is our only sure defense.

SUGGESTED SCRIPTURE READING

James 1:12–15

PRAYER GUIDE

Pray for God's help in times of testing and trials:

- Ask God to help you endure the trial.
- Ask God to help you be victorious over the trial so that you can receive the crown of life.
- Ask God to help you see the way of escape in the trials you face.
- Ask God to help you seek His strength so you will not fall into sin.
- Thank God for His love and for providing you a way of escape.

Our Father's
Surpassing Glory

For Yours is the kingdom and the
power and the glory forever. Amen.
(Matt. 6:13b)

O, for a thousand tongues to sing
   my great Redeemer's praise,
The glories of my God and King,
   the triumphs of His grace.
          —Charles Wesley[1]

*P*rayer magnifies God's character.

"I need all the kids in Mrs. Sweeny's class to line up at this door," the young lady said energetically. She wore a beige safari outfit and a name tag that said, "Jan—Hands-on Science."

She took the group of second graders into a glassed-in room at the back of the children's museum. The room was lined with laboratory tables. A brightly painted, child-sized microscope sat on every table.

"I want two of you at each lab station," said Jan, and the kids chose partners. "Today, we're going to be looking very closely at very small things." After giving the kids some basic instructions about using their microscopes, she continued, "You'll notice there are four slides at your station. Please put slide number one under the scope. Now, look through the eyepiece."

The children began to peer through their microscopes. Some giggled. One boy whispered, "Wow!"

"No talking, now," Jan reminded them. "Has everyone looked at the slide? Good. Okay, what did you see?"

One girl answered, "It's a piece of grass."

"That's right," Jan responded. "Did it look different under the microscope?"

The class agreed that the blade of grass appeared very different. Suddenly, they could see details they had never seen before. For the next thirty minutes, they placed pebbles, seeds, hairs from their own heads, and even a bug under the microscope. Every item amazed them.

Just as a microscope magnifies an object, prayer magnifies God. By this, I do not mean that prayer adds to God's greatness or glory. That would be impossible. Instead, prayer enlarges our understanding of who our Father is. In times of prayer, we begin to know God more profoundly and intensely than ever before.

KNOWING GOD THROUGH PRAYER

In *Knowing God*, J. I. Packer writes, "How can we turn our knowledge *about* God into knowledge *of* God? The rule for doing this is demanding, but simple. It is that we turn each truth that we learn *about* God into matter for meditation *before* God, leading to prayer and praise *to* God."[2]

The last phrase of the Lord's Prayer leads us to adore our glorious God.

Traditionally, the Lord's Prayer concludes with a beautiful doxology—a word of praise to God. This doxology magnifies our heavenly Father by proclaiming, "Yours is the kingdom and the power and the glory forever. Amen." In many modern translations, these lines are placed in brackets or in a footnote at the bottom of the page, for the oldest Greek manuscripts of the New Testament do not include the phrase. The phrase was included as part of the Lord's Prayer, probably for use in the worship and liturgy of the early church. The words are ancient and precious. The ideas presented in this last line of the prayer certainly are found in other places in Scripture. Notably, David prayed in 1 Chronicles 29:11, "Yours, O LORD, is the greatness, the power and the glory, the victory and the majesty, for all that is in heaven and earth is Yours; Yours is the kingdom, O LORD, and You are exalted as head over all."

Prayer draws us close to the surpassing glory of our heavenly Father. The first two parts of this doxology revisit ideas that Jesus presented earlier:

- "Yours is the kingdom." In our study of this prayer, we have already talked about God's kingdom. God calls us to surrender our wills to His will so that His kingdom may come.
- "Yours is the power." We've encountered His power in this prayer—power to provide our daily needs, to forgive our sins, to enable us to forgive others, and to deliver us from Satan.

The last idea presented in this doxology is new: "Yours is the glory." Let us consider God's glory and how prayer magnifies it.

A MAJESTIC WEIGHTINESS

When we ascribe glory to God, we are speaking of His splendor and majesty. The Old Testament word for "glory" is the Hebrew term *chabod*. The word basically means to be heavy or weighty.[3] When *chabod* is used to describe men, it refers to their wealth, dignity, and reputation. In His glory, God possesses a weighty worthiness—a holy heaviness that merits our reverence, fear, and praise.

In *The Legend of Sleepy Hollow*, Washington Irving introduced the world to a homely schoolmaster. The schoolmaster was tall, with narrow shoulders, long arms and legs, hands that dangled a mile out of his sleeves, and feet that looked like shovels. "His head was small, and flat at top, with huge ears, large green glassy eyes, and a long snipe nose, so that it looked like a weather-vane, perched upon his spindle neck, to tell which way the wind blew."[4] This was not a good-looking guy. And he didn't carry much weight of presence, either. The men in town made fun of him, and the ladies mocked his bungling attempts at romance.

Washington Irving picked a name for this character that perfectly suited his personality and appearance: Ichabod Crane. *Ichabod* is a Hebrew name that literally means, "without glory." There wasn't any *chabod* at all in Ichabod. Nothing about him made him worthy of respect.

How unlike Ichabod our God is. He is full of glory. The prophet Habakkuk gave this witness of the majestic weightiness of the Lord: "His glory covered the heavens, and the earth was full of His praise" (Hab. 3:3). All of heaven cannot contain God's glory, and the tongues of the tribes of all earth cannot adequately express the praise He deserves.

King Solomon and the people of Israel experienced the *chabod* of God on the day the temple in Jerusalem was dedicated. The Bible tells us that when the ark of the covenant was brought into the temple and then into the Holy of Holies, a "cloud filled the house of the LORD, so that the priests could not continue ministering because of the cloud; for the glory of the LORD filled the house of the LORD" (1 Kings 8:10–11). The temple was thick with the heaviness of God's presence. Business-as-usual could not continue. Every priest in God's house had to stop what he was doing in reverence to the manifest presence of the living God. By revealing Himself in this way, God showed His acceptance of the new temple and Israel's worship.

To pray, "Yours is the glory, forever," means coming to grips with God's eternal awesomeness and majesty.

When I was boy, there were men at church who never addressed God as *You*, but always as *Thou* or *Thee.* Perhaps they thought it sounded more religious or impressive to mimic the King James Version speech. I can't help thinking, though, that many of those godly men simply wanted to show an unusual respect for God. We don't need to address God with archaic or ornate language. The language of the Lord's Prayer is not the oratory of the temple or the academy but the simple speech of the marketplace and the village square. We *do* need a realization of God's glory. While we can come to God in prayer intimately, we should never come to Him casually. He deserves the greatest respect and adoration we can give Him.

LIFTING THE VEIL

In the New Testament, the word *glory* reveals something else about God's character. While the Hebrew *chabod* talks about God's heaviness, the Greek word for glory, *doxa*, speaks of His light. God's *doxa* has to do with His brightness, brilliance, and radiance. Through His bright and shining glory, God catches the eyes of all who see Him, captures the attention of all who know Him, and captivates the hearts of all who love Him. God's glory reminds us that He is light, and that "in Him is no darkness at all" (1 John 1:5).

As God in flesh, Jesus is the culmination and ultimate demonstration of God's glory. The author of Hebrews describes Jesus as "being the brightness of [God's] glory and the express image of His person" (Heb. 1:3a). God's glory is the unapproachable light in which Jesus dwells (1 Tim. 6:16). We are shown these pictures of Christ's dazzling glory:

- At Jesus's birth, the angelic hosts were illuminated as "the glory of the Lord shone around them" (Luke 2:9).
- Jesus promised that at His return all the earth "will see the Son of Man coming on the clouds of heaven with power and great glory" (Matt. 24:30).
- As he lay dying, the martyr Stephen saw "the glory of God, and Jesus standing at the right hand of God"(Acts 7:55).
- After encountering Jesus on the road to Damascus, Paul said, "I could not see for the glory of that light" (Acts 22:11).

- Jesus led Peter, James, and John to the top of a high mountain. As the three disciples watched, Jesus took on a supernatural appearance that revealed His radiant glory. Matthew writes, "His face shone like the sun, and His clothes became as white as the light" (Matt. 17:2).

Regarding the transfigured Christ he had seen on the mountain, Peter reflected that Jesus "received from God the Father honor and glory when such a voice came to Him from the Excellent Glory: 'This is My beloved Son, in whom I am well pleased.' And we heard this voice which came from heaven when we were with Him on the holy mountain" (2 Peter 1:17–18). John must have been thinking in part of this life-changing event when he wrote, "The Word became flesh and dwelt among us, and we beheld His glory, the glory as of the only begotten of the Father, full of grace and truth" (John 1:14). Those who saw the glory of Jesus were never the same again.

When author Robert Louis Stevenson visited the island country of Samoa, he was invited to speak at an institute where native pastors were trained for ministry. He told a strange story to the students about a fortune-teller who was highly respected as a prophet. He always wore a veil over his face because he claimed that the glory of his face was so great that no one could bear the sight.

Over the years, the veil grew brittle and began to come apart, until the people discovered that they had been tricked. This was a false prophet, who had worn the veil only to conceal his ugliness. Stevenson reminded the students that, no matter how skillfully they might try to cover their blemishes, the veil of their making finally would fall away, showing them as they really were.

We might try to cover our spiritual blotches and disfigurement with a veil of pretend spirituality or sham holiness, but those facades do not fool God. When we enter God's presence in prayer, however, He works to conform us to the image of His Son. In 2 Corinthians 3:18, Paul describes a transformation process that God accomplishes in the life of every believer: "We all, with unveiled face, beholding as in a mirror the glory of the Lord, are being transformed into the same image from glory to glory, just as by the Spirit of the Lord."

God persistently works in our lives through prayer to conform us to the radiance of His Son's glory. Wayne Grudem notes, "There is a brightness, a splendor, or a beauty about the manner of life of a person who deeply loves God, and it is often evident to those around such a person."[5]

JUST TRY TO DESCRIBE HIM

"What is God like?" Children ask such questions, but so have countless Christians through the ages. One can usually find adjectives and metaphors to adequately describe the characteristics and behavior of another man or a woman. Describing God is substantially more difficult, because He is beyond our words. Language and thought fail us when we try to understand what God is like. Yet, as A. W. Tozer observed, what comes into our minds when we think about God is the most important thing about us.[6]

"What is God like?" The most satisfactory (and most biblical) answer is, "God is glorious!" When the Bible talks about God's glory, it does not simply have in view one characteristic of His being or essence. Glory emanates from the nature and presence of His entire person. Glory describes each of His attributes. When we pray, "Yours is the glory," we can reflect on any of the truths about our heavenly Father, for example,

- *He is self-existent.* All created things have a beginning and a cause, but not God.
- *He is self-sufficient.* God created all there is—not out of any need that He has—but simply because it pleases Him.
- *He is eternal.* For God, yesterday, today, and tomorrow are all "now."
- *He is infinite.* Everything about God is without limit. He knows no bounds.

- *He is changeless.* God has no need to change, because He is perfect. He shines with unflickering perfection.
- *He is omniscient.* God knows everything. He is never surprised and never amazed.
- *He is omnipotent.* God has all power. There is nothing too difficult for Him to do.
- *He is all-wise.* God sees everything in focus. His wisdom is without flaw.
- *He is transcendent.* God is above all things. He actively sustains His creation, but stands apart from it.
- *He is omnipresent.* He is fully and always everywhere. Though He is transcendent above us, He is ever present with us.
- *He is faithful.* We may be unfaithful to Him due to fear, weakness, or our own desires, but God will never waver in His devotion to us.
- *He is good.* Because God is good, He takes pleasure in the happiness of His people.
- *He is just.* God's perfect righteousness will not leave the guilty unpunished.
- *He is merciful.* Through Christ, God extends compassion to those who have offended His justice.
- *He is gracious.* God offers eternal and abundant life as a gift of His grace.
- *He is loving.* God's love is personal, intimate, and transforming, having no beginning or end.
- *He is holy.* God is completely different from humanity. While we may fear God's power and admire His wisdom, we cannot even imagine His holiness.
- *God is sovereign.* God rules His creation with absolute sovereignty. He alone governs the universe He has made.

FOR HIS GLORY ALONE

At the beginning of each of his manuscripts, Johann Sebastian Bach set the initials, "J. J.," for *"Jesu Juva,"* or "Jesus, help me." At the end of each piece, he wrote, "S. D. G" for *"Soli Deo Gloria,"* which means "To the glory of God alone." Writing those initials on each piece was more than simply a ritual or a habit for the great musician. J. S. Bach consciously offered each composition to God. He once said, "The aim and final reason for all music should be nothing else than the glory of God."[7]

If God's glory is the aim of music, certainly it must be the aim of prayer. Through prayer, God shows more of His glory. He magnifies Himself in our hearts so that we better understand who He is and what He is like.

SUGGESTED SCRIPTURE READING

1 Chronicles 29:10–15

PRAYER GUIDE

As you pray, bless the Lord as David did:

- Praise God for being our Father.
- Praise God for His greatness, power, and glory.
- Praise God for His victory and majesty.
- Praise God for creating the heavens and the earth.
- Praise God for reigning over all.
- Praise God for His power, might, and strength.
- Praise God for His holiness.
- Praise God for providing everything you need.
- Praise His holy name.

Day 28

MAKING THE LORD'S PRAYER YOUR PRAYER

What we call "the Lord's Prayer" is not *really* the Lord's prayer. Just about every commentary or book on the Lord's Prayer includes such a statement. I've resisted saying it until now, but it still needs to be said. The Lord's Prayer is a model Jesus provided, not a prayer that He actually prayed. Jesus would never have prayed to be forgiven, since He never sinned. There are other prayers the Lord prayed, such as His prayer in Gethsemane or His high priestly prayer in John 17. The Lord's Prayer is an outline for prayer that Christ offered for His disciples.

The Lord's Prayer is *our* prayer. It's a perfect pattern for how to pray.

SUGGESTED SCRIPTURE READING

Matthew 6:9–13

PRAYER GUIDE

We have been taking this prayer apart. Now, let's put it back together. How can you make the Lord's Prayer a part of your prayer life?

- *Begin by worshipping God.* "Our Father in heaven, hallowed be Your name" (Matt. 6:9).
- *Surrender to God's priorities for your life.* "Your kingdom come. Your will be done on earth as it is in heaven" (v. 10).
- *Bring your daily needs to God.* "Give us this day our daily bread" (v. 11).
- *Seek His forgiveness for sins you have committed.* "And forgive us our debts, as we forgive our debtors" (v. 12).
- *Ask for His protection from the tests and temptations of life.* "And do not lead us into temptation, but deliver us from the evil one" (v. 13a).
- *End by glorifying Him.* "For Yours is the kingdom and the power and glory forever. Amen" (v. 13b).

CRUCIAL QUESTIONS
ABOUT PRAYER

Why should I pray?
Who can pray?
When should I pray?
How should I pray?
To whom should I pray?
Does God always answer my prayers?
How can I pray for others?
Should I pray for healing?
How should I teach my child to pray?
How can I pray to become a Christian?

WHY SHOULD I PRAY?

George McDonald was one of many Christians who have asked the question *Why pray?* After all, if God loves us and knows everything we need, what's the point in praying at all? Can't God accomplish what He wants to achieve in our lives and the world apart from our prayers? Can't He meet the needs in our lives whether we pray or not? These are legitimate questions.

McDonald answered his own question this way:

> What if the main object in God's idea of prayer be the supplying of our great, our endless need—the need of himself? What if the good of all our smaller and lower needs lies in this, that they help drive us to God? Communion with God is the one need of the soul beyond all other needs; prayer is the beginning of that communion.[1]

The Bible provides a number of reasons that believers should seek communion with God through prayer.

1. God Invites Us to Pray.

The God who created the universe and who sustains all of His creation moment by moment not only *allows* us to call on Him in prayer, He *commands* us to pray. He invites us to bring our needs to Him in prayer. "Cast your burden on the LORD, and He shall sustain you; He shall never permit the righteous to be moved" (Ps. 55:22). "Therefore humble yourselves under the mighty hand of God, that He may exalt you in due time, casting all your care upon Him, for He cares for you" (1 Peter 5:6–7).

God longs for us to know Him. He desires to hear from us so that we will understand more about His character and nature. He uses prayer to draw us closer.

2. Jesus Prayed.

Jesus, God's own Son, prayed extensively during His earthly ministry. The gospel records show that He made prayer a priority. Jesus spent extended times alone with God in prayer. "And when He had sent the multitudes away, He went up on the mountain by Himself to pray. Now when evening came, He was alone there" (Matt. 14:23). He also took time in the best part of His busy day to pray. "Now in the morning, having risen a long while before daylight, He went out and departed to a solitary place; and there He prayed" (Mark 1:35).

If Jesus depended on prayer in His communion with His Father, how much more should we who follow Him spend time daily with God!

3. God Hears and Answers Our Prayers.

God is never too busy to listen to us when we call. He promises that He will hear our prayers and answer them. "Now this is the confidence that we have in Him, that if we ask anything according to His will, He hears us" (1 John 5:14). "The righteous cry out, and the LORD hears, and delivers them out of all their troubles" (Ps. 34:17). "Evening and morning and at noon I will pray, and cry aloud, and He shall hear my voice" (Ps. 55:17). Though God does not always answer our prayers the way we might have anticipated, He answers, nonetheless. And He uses the time we spend before Him in prayer both to conform our will to His own and to help us understand His ways.

4. Prayer Nurtures Us Spiritually.

A child grows physically by eating right, exercising regularly, and getting plenty of rest. The developing child grows mentally by being challenged to develop thinking skills and to master new areas of learning. A child of God grows spiritually by spending time in the presence of the heavenly Father. Through prayer and meditation on Scripture, God cultivates our spiritual lives. God's Word tells us, "Draw near to God and He will draw near to you" (James 4:8). Prayer brings us close to God.

Whether the story is true or an invention of piano teachers, the legend runs that a concert pianist was asked whether she practiced every day. "I try to," she answered. "If I go a month without practicing, my audience notices it. If I go a week without practicing, the music critics notice it. But if I go a day without practicing, I notice it." In the same way, God is the one who notices when a believer goes a day without praying, but eventually others will notice as well.

5. Prayer Empowers Us to Witness.

We are not ready to talk to other people about God until we have first talked to God about other people. Through prayer, we ask God to prepare us to share the good news of Jesus, even as God must prepare unbelievers to hear the gospel. Paul prayed for the souls of men and women. He wrote that his "heart's desire and prayer to God for Israel is that they may be saved" (Rom. 10:1). His burden for souls moved Paul to encourage believers "that supplications, prayers, intercessions, and giving of thanks be made for all men," knowing that God "desires all men to be saved and to come to the knowledge of the truth" (1 Tim. 2:1, 4).

6. Prayer Is a Way of Worshipping God.

God's Word commands, "Come, let us worship and bow down; let us kneel before the LORD our Maker" (Ps. 95:6). Prayer shows God how much He is worth to us. We acknowledge His power and His might. Through prayer, we come to God, saying, "I will praise You, O LORD, with my whole heart; I will tell of all Your marvelous works. I will be glad and rejoice in You; I will sing praise to Your name, O Most High" (Ps. 9:1–2). Prayer is a way of praising our God who is eminently worthy to be worshipped and adored.

7. Guidance Comes in Prayer.

In a confusing world, God offers leadership and wisdom through prayer. Imagine that you had an appointment for a ten-minute meeting with the head of a nation. Would you be more interested in what you had to tell this ruler, or in what the leader might want to tell you? Probably the time would be better spent hearing what the leader had to say. In the same way, prayer should be more about listening than about talking.

Too often, we are so intent on telling God about our needs that we neglect to hear His voice. God says, "I will bring the blind by a way they did not know; I will lead them in paths they have not known. I will make darkness light before them, and crooked places straight. These things I will do for them, and not forsake them" (Isa. 42:16). As we pray, we can ask for the same guidance from God that the psalmist wanted when he prayed, "Lead me in Your truth and teach me, for You are the God of my salvation; on You I wait all the day" (Ps. 25:5).

WHO CAN PRAY?

Who can pray? The short answer to that question is *anyone*. Anyone from any religious background—or with no religious background at all—can form the words of a prayer. People pray instinctively at times of sorrow or danger, even if they are calling out to gods fashioned in their own imaginations. Anyone can pray. But the short answer doesn't get at the heart of the matter.

We might rephrase the question, "Whose prayers does God hear?" Even that question has an elusive answer. God hears the prayers of everyone, since He is all-knowing and all-present. He is aware of the prayers of a Buddhist or a Muslim or even an atheist—if the atheist should choose to pray. However, God is under no more obligation to honor the prayer of a Buddhist or a Muslim than He would be obligated to answer a prayer offered to Mickey Mouse or the Man in the Moon. God is not the god of Buddhism or Islam.

When we ask, *Who can pray?* we're really asking, *Who has access to God in prayer?* Who is on praying terms with God? Who has the right to call on His name and expect Him to answer? God's Word provides conditions we must meet if we are to call on God in prayer.

1. We Can Pray When We Call on the True and Living God.

The psalmist writes, "Give ear to my words, O LORD, consider my meditation. Give heed to the voice of my cry, my King and my God, for to You I will pray" (Ps. 5:1–2). According to Scripture, prayer does not involve merely talking to oneself for therapeutic or motivational reasons. Nor does authentic prayer consist of sending out requests to some vaguely defined "higher power." Instead, prayer is communication with the only true God.

God has revealed Himself in history as the "the God of Abraham, the God of Isaac, and the God of Jacob" (Exod. 3:6). He revealed Himself ultimately in Jesus Christ, "His Son, whom He has appointed heir of all things, through whom also He made the worlds" (Heb. 1:2). Only when we pray to God as He is revealed in Christian Scripture do our prayers have the promise of being heard and answered.

God illustrated this truth powerfully when Elijah challenged the prophets of Baal on Mount Carmel. The prophets of the false god cried out to their deity all morning long. Frustrated at Baal's silence, they began to jump up and down on the altar they had made. They even cut themselves with knives in order to get their god's attention. But there was "no voice; no one answered, no one paid attention" (1 Kings 18:29b).

To pray to any god other than the living God revealed in the Bible is like sending an e-mail message to an account that doesn't exist, or dialing an imaginary telephone number, or sending a letter to a fictional address. No one receives the message and no one answers because no one is there.

How different the situation is when we call on the Lord. After the prophets of Baal had attempted unsuccessfully to contact their deity, Elijah simply called out to the Lord, and God answered his prayer by sending fire from heaven. The people of Israel fell on their faces and proclaimed, "The LORD, He is God! The LORD, He is God!" (1 Kings 18:39).

2. We Can Pray When We Have a Relationship with God.

Jesus said, "I am the way, the truth, and the life. No one comes to the Father except through Me" (John 14:6). In our pluralistic age, it seems offensively narrow-minded to say, "Only through faith in Jesus can a person be saved. Only through a relationship with Jesus can a person come to God in prayer." But Jesus has made exclusive claims. He is not merely one way among many ways or one truth among other truths. He is the only way, the only truth, and the only life, and no one comes to God the Father apart from Him.

God's Word affirms that "there is one God and one Mediator between God and men, the Man Christ Jesus" (1 Tim. 2:5). The wonderful truth of the gospel is that all people in all places from all backgrounds can know God personally through Jesus Christ. He came to die for the sins of the whole world (1 John 2:2). All people *can* come to God through Jesus, and all people *must* come to God through Jesus. Through Jesus alone we can call on God in prayer.

3. We Can Pray When Our Hearts Are Clean Before God.

God's Word is clear that our hearts must be clean when we bring our requests to God. The psalmist writes, "If I regard iniquity in my heart, the Lord will not hear" (Ps. 66:18). "Who may ascend into the hill of the LORD? Or who may stand in His holy place? He who has clean hands and a pure heart" (Ps. 24:3–4a). Confession of sin is an important part of prayer because cleansing opens the way for us to make requests and offer worship to God. Just as the omission of one ingredient in a cake recipe can result in a failure, so the omission of confessing known sin can result in prayer failure. Before we come to God with praise or petitions, we must come seeking His cleansing.

4. We Can Pray When We Have Forgiven Others.

Jesus reminded His disciples that an unforgiving person should not expect to be heard by God in prayer. "And whenever you stand praying," Jesus said, "if you have anything against anyone, forgive him, that your Father in heaven may also forgive you your trespasses. But if you do not forgive, neither will your Father in heaven forgive your trespasses" (Mark 11:25–26). We are not on praying terms with God if we are bitter, angry, or unforgiving toward another person. One of the things that God's Spirit does when we pray is to convict us of unforgiveness and other sins so that our relationships with God and others can be restored.

5. We Can Pray When We Are Placing Trust in God.

Our hearts must not only be clean when we come to God in prayer; they must also be full of faith in Him. Jesus said, "And whatever things you ask in prayer, believing, you will receive" (Matt. 21:22). Believing in God as we pray means trusting that He is able to answer our prayer, that His answer is always the best, and that He has the sovereign right to answer as He sees fit. Real prayer involves taking God seriously and placing our faith fully in Him. God's Word reminds us, "But without faith it is impossible to please Him, for he who comes to God must believe that He is, and that He is a rewarder of those who diligently seek Him" (Heb. 11:6).

WHEN SHOULD I PRAY?

"To everything there is a season," Ecclesiastes 3:1 tells us, "and a time for every purpose under heaven." Whether it is time for living or dying, planting or harvesting, gaining or losing, laughing or weeping—prayer fits the moment. Prayer belongs to every season of life.

The Bible presents four major principles concerning when we should pray.

1. We Should Maintain an Attitude of Prayer Continually.

God's Word contains a number of instructions for believers to keep a mind-set of unending prayer. The psalmist writes, "O LORD, God of my salvation, I have cried out day and night before You" (Ps. 88:1). Jesus taught that believers "always ought to pray and not lose heart" (Luke 18:1). Paul indicated that he was always praying for his fellow believers (Col. 1:3), and he called for Christians to "continue earnestly in prayer, being vigilant in it with thanksgiving" (4:2). Perhaps the most urgent plea for continual prayer, however, is the simple scriptural command, "Pray without ceasing" (1 Thess. 5:17). The Greek adverb translated "without ceasing" was used to describe something continual and persistent, such as a hacking cough that won't go away. Paul was instructing his readers to continue praying whenever possible.

To see how continual prayer works in life, imagine taking a cross-country trip alongside someone. During the long hours or days on the road, the two of you are continually chatting with each other. There will be interruptions in dialogue. You might listen to the radio for a while. You stop at a shop and go in different directions. A cell phone call might interrupt the dialogue. But over the length the trip, you and your traveling companion are engaged in conversation. If the two of you made the entire journey without speaking, or if you only spoke when forced to do so, you probably dislike one another.

When we have a loving relationship with God, we will live in continual prayer. Though interruptions will come throughout the day, we will always be engaged in an ongoing conversation with Him. We will say with David, "I will bless the LORD at all times; His praise shall continually be in my mouth" (Ps. 34:1).

2. We Should Pursue the Discipline of Prayer Daily.

In addition to maintaining an attitude that prayer is continual, God desires that we set aside specific focused times of prayer to Him. David wrote, "Evening and morning and at noon I will pray, and cry aloud, and He shall hear my voice" (Ps. 55:17). Many believers have used those three times—evening, morning, and noon—as occasions for scheduled prayer. The prophet Daniel, for example, "knelt down on his knees three times [a] day, and prayed and gave thanks before his God, as was his custom since early days" (Dan. 6:10). Making time in your schedule for prayer is essential for growth as a Christian and closeness to God.

Morning prayers offer a great opportunity to worship and praise our Creator, to acknowledge Jesus as our Master, and to ask for the filling of the Holy Spirit for that day. In the morning, we can lift up concerns of our day and make requests for others who are facing immediate challenges.

At noon, we can pray for wisdom and direction for decisions, listening to God's voice as we meditate on the Scriptures. We can ask for opportunities to share the gospel with others. We can pray for our pastors, leaders, and friends.

Evening prayers should include a time of personal examination, as we ask, "Is there anything in me, God, that displeases You?" As the Holy Spirit shows us the sins we have committed, we can confess them and find forgiveness. We can also ask for strength in Christ to overcome those sins. Prayer in the evening hours gives us opportunity to end the day as we began it, with thanksgiving and praise.

3. We Should Look for Opportunities for Prayer Constantly.

"Is anyone among you suffering? Let him pray. Is anyone cheerful? Let him sing psalms" (James 5:13). God encourages us to call on Him in all circumstances. As we go about our lives, we should be on the alert for opportunities to call out to God. Make it a habit to pray anytime the Holy Spirit prompts. You may pause to pray while working or while driving down the highway. In family activities, stop and pray often. If possible, pray immediately when someone gives a prayer request. Throughout the day, be on the lookout for times to pray.

4. We Should Pray with Others Regularly.

Though prayer is intensely personal, it also has a corporate dimension. In the earliest days of the church, the Bible says that believers "all continued with one accord in prayer and supplication" (Acts 1:14). As a result of their steadfast prayers, these believers experienced supernatural power. Typical group prayer meetings are often dull and lifeless because the majority of Christians in the group do not have flourishing personal prayer lives. As a result, communal prayers are empty and powerless.

God has something greater in mind when Christians pray together. Jesus told His disciples, "If two of you agree on earth concerning anything that they ask, it will be done for them by My Father in heaven. For where two or three are gathered together in My name, I am there in the midst of them" (Matt. 18:19–20). While this promise was made primarily in the context of church discipline (see vv. 15–18), it holds implications for other sorts of corporate prayers. As we come together in prayer as believers, we can claim the presence of Christ in our midst. We can trust Christ to direct us in our prayers because He is head of the church. As we surrender to His lordship in prayer, He will bring our prayers into harmony with the Father and in agreement with one another.[2]

HOW SHOULD I PRAY?

"All you need to do to learn to pray is to pray."[3] Those words by missionary Wesley Duewel show insight. While reading a book on prayer, taking a class on it, or listening to exhortation to prayer in a sermon can all be good, the main thing is to spend time in conversation with God. One can listen to a musician play beautiful music for a year without learning anything about how to play the instrument personally. To learn to pray is to practice prayer.

It's not true, however, that prayer ever comes naturally and spontaneously or that believers need no training in how to pray. If prayer came naturally, God would not have taken so much space in His Word to teach us how to pray. As we seek a more purposeful prayer life, there are some biblical principles to keep in mind regarding patterns for prayer, postures for prayer, and preparation for prayer.

1. Patterns for Prayer

Because prayer is conversation between you and God, you should not feel as though you need to have a checklist of things to include in your prayers. Too much rigidity can drain your prayer life of its energy and turn your time into empty ritual. Even so, there is value in thinking about what elements to include in prayers. Especially for Christians who are trying to begin a more disciplined prayer life, using a pattern or outline can keep our prayers from meandering meaninglessly and can help us to stay focused as we talk to God.

One practical pattern is to pray using the A-C-T-S acronym. Let's consider each part of this pattern:

- *Adoration.* We adore God, worshipping and honoring Him with hearts and lips. Prayer activities can include meditating on a psalm or a hymn text.
- *Confession.* The Holy Spirit reveals areas in our lives where we need God's cleansing. As He shows us those areas, we ask God's forgiveness and seek His strength to have victory over those sins in the future.
- *Thanksgiving.* God blesses those who have thankful hearts. Prayer can express gratitude to God for daily blessings and promises, forgiveness through Christ, and our relationship in the Savior.
- *Supplication.* Prayer time should include requests for our own needs and for the needs of others. As we pray about our concerns and for wisdom and guidance, we know that nothing is too large for Him to handle nor too small for Him to care about.

The Lord's Prayer is above all a pattern for prayer. While we have studied this prayer extensively, we should look for a moment at its overall pattern. The prayer can be divided into six sections:

1. *Worship.* "Our Father in heaven, hallowed be Your name" (Matt. 6:9).
2. *Surrender.* "Your kingdom come. Your will be done on earth as it is in heaven" (v. 10).
3. *Trust.* "Give us this day our daily bread" (v. 11).
4. *Seeking His forgiveness.* "And forgive us our debts, as we forgive our debtors" (v. 12).
5. *Requesting His strength.* "And do not lead us into temptation, but deliver us from the evil one" (v. 13a).

6. *Acknowledging His glory.* "For Yours is the kingdom and the power and the glory forever. Amen" (v. 13b).

2. Postures for Prayer

A common prayer practice is to bow the head, fold the hands, and close the eyes. While this practice is appropriate, nowhere in Scripture does God command such a posture. Scripture depicts God's people praying in a variety of physical positions.

Standing is the traditional Jewish posture for prayer. It is mentioned in both the Old and New Testaments. Abraham stood when he interceded for Sodom (Gen. 18:22). In Nehemiah 9:2, the Israelites "stood and confessed their sins and the iniquities of their fathers." The prophet Jeremiah stood to pray for God to withhold His wrath from his enemies (Jer. 18:20). Jesus assumed that His disciples would stand when they prayed (Mark 11:25).

Kneeling or lying down in prayer is mentioned, especially when people were praying in extreme situations or making urgent requests. Daniel habitually prayed on his knees in his room (Dan. 6:10), as did King Solomon at the dedication of the temple (1 Kings 8:54). Paul indicated that he bowed his knees when he prayed (Eph. 3:14). In Gethsemane, Jesus both knelt when He prayed (Luke 22:41–44) and threw His face down on the ground (Mark 14:35–36).

Spreading the palms in prayer is frequent in the Old Testament. By praying in this position, petitioners may have suggested their desire for God to fill their hands with the requests they were making. Moses prayed with outstretched hands when he asked for one of the plagues to cease (Exod. 9:29). Solomon did so before the altar (1 Kings 8:22). In Psalm 28:2, David wrote of praying with lifted hands: "I lift up my hands toward Your holy sanctuary." Paul commended this posture: "I desire therefore that the men pray everywhere, lifting up holy hands" (1 Tim. 2:8).

Other prayer postures include *sitting* (2 Sam. 7:18), *bowing the head* (Gen. 24:26), and *lifting the eyes* (John 17:1).

We might assume that our posture in prayer is insignificant. The

Bible allows us to pray in many different physical positions. We recognize that the most important thing is the posture of the heart when we pray. The knee can't be bowed while the heart remains defiant. Our physical posture, however, may convey something significant about our expectations when we pray. Our outward position can affect our inner attitudes. As you pray, you may feel God directing you to stand, to walk, to kneel, to sit, or even to lie down.

3. Preparation for Prayer

Finding a place. Jesus told His disciples, "When you pray, go into your room, and when you have shut your door, pray to your Father" (Matt. 6:6a). The King James Bible translates the word *room* as *closet*, which has led some Christians to go into an actual closet to pray. The word Jesus used simply means "a place of privacy." Whether you pray in the corner of a bedroom, on the deck in your backyard, in a chair in your family room, or in the smallest room of your house, it is helpful to designate a special location for meeting with God. Having a specific place where you pray also serves as testimony to your family about the priority of prayer in your life. The best place for prayer is somewhere quiet and accessible.

Setting a time. Just as you will benefit from selecting a particular place for prayer, you will also find it advantageous to pick a regular prayer time. Select a time that allows you to be at your best as you come to God. Don't give God the scraps of your day, when your mind is preoccupied with other things or when your body is exhausted. Instead, find a time of day when you are alert and able to focus on God, a time when you know you will be readily available. Then make an appointment to meet God at that time. We are usually careful to keep appointments with other people. We should be even more diligent to honor appointments with God in prayer.

Meditating on God's Word. When we pray we read the Bible in order to prepare our hearts to hear from Him. D. Martyn Lloyd-Jones observed that starting to pray without meditating on God's Word is like starting a car when it is cold. Meditating on a short portion of

God's Word at the start of prayer will help get rid of coldness that may have developed in your spirit.[4]

Fasting. Sometimes, believers go without food or drink for an extended period in order to seek God in prayer. The Bible indicates that people fasted when confronted with God's judgment (Joel 1:14; 2:12); when experiencing national calamities (2 Sam. 1:12); when undergoing personal suffering (Ps. 35:13; 2 Sam. 12:16); and when commissioning believers to proclaim the gospel (Acts 13:3). Fasting was an integral part of the spiritual lives of many in the Bible, including Moses (Exod. 34:28), Elijah (1 Kings 19:8), and the Lord Jesus (Matt. 4:2). When we are committed to prayer, there will be occasions when God will lead us to fast. We want to be sensitive and obedient to His leadership.

TO WHOM SHOULD I PRAY?

The lady came to me with a serious look on her face. She had a question that was bothering her deeply. "Is it okay for me to pray to Jesus or to the Holy Spirit," she asked, "or should I only pray to God the Father?" Such questions have come to the mind of most Christians on occasion. Is there some sort of spiritual etiquette to follow when we address God in prayer? Does it make a difference whether we begin our prayers, *Dear Father, Dear Jesus,* or *Dear Holy Spirit?*

Part of the richness of God's being is the reality of the Trinity. The beautiful yet mysterious doctrine of the Triune God—which says that the one true God exists and has revealed Himself in three persons—is beyond our ability to fully comprehend. It may be the most difficult thought the human mind has ever been asked to grasp. We accept by faith the biblical truth that God is one (Deut. 6:4), and that He is eternally Father (1 Peter 1:2), Son (Col. 1:15–17), and Holy Spirit (Acts 5:3–4).

According to Scripture, each member of the Trinity plays a part in our prayers. In theological terms we can differentiate how the Godhead interacts with us in prayer.

God the Father receives our prayers. Jesus instructed us to pray to the Father. He told His disciples, "But you, when you pray, go into your room, and when you have shut your door, pray to your Father who is in the secret place; and your Father who sees in secret will reward you openly" (Matt. 6:6). Praying to our Father in heaven reminds us that God is not cold or impersonal. He cares for us, and—through our faith in Jesus—He receives us as His dear children.

God the Son authorizes our prayers. The prayers we lift to the Father are validated by our relationship with Jesus Christ. It is through Him that we have access to God (1 Tim. 2:5). Through His shed blood on the cross, we are able to come without apprehension to God's throne of grace in prayer (Heb. 4:14–16). Jesus has authorized us as believers to make requests to the Father in His name (John 14:13–14). Furthermore, Jesus is our partner in prayer, for Scripture tells us that He intercedes for believers continually (Rom. 8:34; Heb. 7:25).

God the Holy Spirit interprets our prayers. It is the Spirit of God living in us who helps us pray to God the Father (Rom. 8:15). God's Word tells us that the Holy Spirit intercedes for us, speaking to God on our behalf when we do not know how to pray. "Likewise the Spirit also helps in our weaknesses. For we do not know what we should pray for as we ought, but the Spirit Himself makes intercession for us with groanings which cannot be uttered" (v. 26).

Because the three persons of the Trinity are fully and equally God, Christians can pray to Jesus or to the Holy Spirit and know that their prayers are heard and answered. Indeed, one of the most learned theologians I have ever known almost always began his public prayers, "Dear Lord Jesus." However, the scriptural pattern established by Jesus in the Lord's Prayer is for believers to call on the Father as we pray. For this reason, our prayers should be directed to the Father in the name of the Lord Jesus Christ through the ministry of the Holy Spirit.

DOES GOD ALWAYS ANSWER MY PRAYERS?

"Our Lord never referred to unanswered prayer."[5] This statement by Oswald Chambers may seem startling, but it's true. Jesus taught that prayers are always answered: "For everyone who asks receives, and he who seeks finds, and to him who knocks it will be opened" (Luke 11:10).

God promises always to answer prayer. So, why does our experience sometimes tell us otherwise? Over the years, I have listened when people asked:

- Why didn't God answer my prayers when my baby was sick?
- Why didn't God hear my prayers for my marriage?
- Why didn't God answer my prayer for my career?
- Why didn't God hear our prayers for our unborn child?

Many sincere Christians who want to take prayer seriously are troubled and disappointed by prayers that seem to go unanswered. As we examine the Bible, we discover some insights about the way God responds to the prayers of His people.

The Answer "No"

One reason we feel let down when our prayers aren't granted is that we have forgotten that *no* is a real answer to prayer. God promises to answer when we call on Him, but He does not always agree to answer the way we would prefer. James and John, two of Jesus's closest disciples, came to the Lord with the same attitude that many Christians have. They said, "Teacher, we want You to do for us whatever we ask." Graciously, Jesus gave them opportunity to make a request. Then, they asked to sit at the Lord's right hand and left hand in His glory. When Jesus refused their request, James and John continued following Him (Mark 10:35–38). David fasted and pleaded for God to spare the life of the first child Bathsheba bore him, but God answered *no*. Rather than responding with bitterness, he accepted God's answer and kept serving the Lord (2 Sam. 12:15–23). The biblical record is clear; sometimes God gives a negative answer to the prayers of His people.

If God were simply to fulfill every wish of our hearts, two problems would arise. First, He would have to give up His sovereignty. Our prayers would rule the universe instead of God, if He were obligated to do whatever we asked. Second, if God promised to answer *yes* to all our prayers, we would find ourselves regretting many things we had requested. We all have prayed for foolish or short-sighted things. God is not like some genie in a bottle who will grant us our wishes even when they would harm us. In His wisdom, God answers *no* to some prayers. Theologian P. T. Forsyth made this profound observation: "We shall come one day to a heaven where we shall gratefully know that God's refusals were sometimes the true answer to our truest prayers."[6]

Prayer Barriers

God's Word reveals several obstacles that can hinder our prayers. When these things are present in our lives, God is unlikely to respond to our prayers with positive answers. Barriers to prayer include:

1. *Sin and disobedience.* "Behold, the LORD's hand is not short-ened, that it cannot save; nor His ear heavy, that it cannot hear. But your iniquities have separated you from your God; and your sins have hidden His face from you, so that He will not hear" (Isa. 59:1–2). "If I regard iniquity in my heart, the Lord will not hear me" (Ps. 66:18). If we refuse to confess and forsake known sin in our lives, iniquity will create a barrier in our communication with God.

   Not only can sin in our own lives keep God from answer-ing *yes* to our prayers, but sin in the lives of other people can also hinder a prayer. A spouse, for instance, may be praying fervently for a marriage to be reconciled, but the other spouse is unwilling to move from stark rebellion against God's will for marriage, so the marriage may still disintegrate. Similarly, a godly parent may pray for the salvation of a child, but the prayer will be answered *no* so long as the child is shaking a fist at God.

2. *Selfish motives.* "You ask and do not receive, because you ask amiss, that you may spend it on your pleasures" (James 4:3). God knows our hearts and our motives. When we are asking for something merely to satisfy our own selfish desires, we can expect God to answer *no.*

3. *Pride.* "God resists the proud, but gives grace to the humble" (James 4:6). God opposes a proud heart. Christians who presumptuously come to God in prayer with pride and haughtiness will not receive a positive answer.

4. *Unbelief.* "But let him ask in faith, with no doubting, for he who doubts is like a wave of the sea driven and tossed by the wind. For let not that man suppose that he will receive anything from the Lord" (James 1:6–7). Genuine prayer involves trusting that God hears and answers. Prayers offered without faith in God are nothing more than wishful thinking.

5. *Unforgiveness.* "For if you forgive men their trespasses, your heavenly Father will also forgive you. But if you do not forgive men their trespasses, neither will your Father forgive your trespasses" (Matt. 6:14–15). Jesus told His followers that an unforgiving spirit keeps God from hearing and answering our prayers.

6. *Misplaced priorities.* We commit idolatry when we allow other people or things to reign in our hearts instead of God. God says, "These men have set up their idols in their hearts, and put before them that which causes them to stumble into iniquity. Should I let Myself be inquired of at all by them?" (Ezek. 14:3). Christians who have not given Jesus first place in their lives may find their prayers hindered.

7. *Praying outside of God's will.* "Now this is the confidence that we have in Him, that if we ask anything according to His will, He hears us" (1 John 5:14). Here is a mystery of prayer. We know that prayer moves God to act. At least that's what it looks like from our perspective. We also know that God answers positively only prayers that are in keeping with His will. Sometimes, it is not within God's will to heal a sick person

or to deliver a believer from a painful situation. Christians throughout the ages have discovered, however, that God uses prayer to bring our desires into line with His own and to help us accept His will with joy.

A Delayed Answer

Not only does God sometimes deny our requests, He also may choose to delay an answer. God may withhold an answer to a prayer because the timing is not right, or He may delay because He knows that we aren't ready for His answer. Waiting on God's answer can be excruciating. We tend to become impatient when we have asked God repeatedly about a need or a problem and are forced to wait on an answer.

When an answer to prayer seems slow in coming, believers must remember that God's response is delayed only from our human perspective. From God's perspective, His answers always come right on time. We also must remember that God is working in us between the time of our request and the time of His answer.

"If you abide in Me, and My words abide in you," Jesus said, "you will ask what you desire, and it shall be done for you" (John 15:7). To abide is to wait patiently. As we abide in Christ we become more intimately aware of His presence and His ways. When we abide in Him, Jesus teaches us how to trust in His timing and how to pray according to His will. "We must be careful not to take delays in prayer for denials," wrote C. H. Spurgeon. "God's long-dated bills will be punctually honored; we must not suffer Satan to shake our confidence in the God of truth by pointing to our unanswered prayers."[7]

HOW CAN I PRAY FOR OTHERS?

"For though we walk in the flesh, we do not war according to the flesh. For the weapons of our warfare are not carnal but mighty in God for pulling down strongholds" (2 Cor. 10:3–4). Intercessory prayer is a mighty weapon and a high call for any believer. One of the delights of the Christian life is the privilege of praying for other people. Within the body of Christ, we all have different gifts and areas of service, but God can use every believer in the ministry of intercessory prayer. The greatest contribution you can make to another human being's life is to pray for that person.

Intercessory Prayer in Scripture

The word *intercession* literally means "to go between." Intercessory prayer involves going to God on behalf of someone else. Intercessory prayer is seen at work often in Scripture. As God's priests, Aaron and his sons were commanded to intercede for the people of Israel (Num. 6:23). David called for God's people to pray for the peace of Jerusalem (Ps. 122:6). God compared righteous intercessors who prayed for Israel to watchmen on the walls of Jerusalem (Isa. 62:6). Paul urged believers that "supplications, prayers, intercessions, and giving of thanks be made for all men" (1 Tim. 2:1). Examples of intercession include:

- Abraham's prayers on behalf of the cities of Sodom and Gomorrah (Gen. 18:23–32).
- Moses's intercession for Pharaoh during the plagues (Exod. 8–9), for the Israelites after they had sinned with the golden calf (32:11–14, 31–34), and for Miriam when she rebelled (Num. 12:13).
- Samuel's prayers for Israel to be delivered from the hands of Philistines (1 Sam. 7:5–12).
- Elijah's prayer for the Sidonian widow's son to be raised from the dead (1 Kings 17:20–23).
- Elisha's prayer for the Shunamite woman's son (2 Kings 4:33–36).
- Peter's prayer for the restoration of Tabitha's life (Acts 9:40).
- Paul's intercession for Publius (Acts 28:8).

By far the most significant instance of intercessory prayer recorded in Scripture is called the "high priestly prayer" of Jesus (John 17). This prayer, offered to the Father on the night before Jesus was crucified, is the longest of the Lord's recorded prayers. He prays first for Himself (vv. 1–5), then for His disciples (vv. 6–19), and finally for future believers (vv. 20–26). As He intercedes, Jesus asks for believers to persevere (vv. 10–12), to have joy (v. 13), to be sanctified (vv. 14–19), to be unified (vv. 20–23), to be with Him in glory (vv. 24–25), and to be filled with God's love (v. 26).

Not only did Jesus intercede for believers before His death, the Bible also teaches that Jesus continues to make unending intercession for us in heaven today. "It is Christ who died, and furthermore is also risen, who is even at the right hand of God, who also makes intercession for us" (Rom. 8:34). Through His present work of intercession, Jesus gives us grace to overcome temptation, to be forgiven of sins, and to be strengthened for victorious living. Jesus Christ stands before the throne of God on our behalf. Additionally, the Holy Spirit also intercedes for believers (v. 26).

"I Am Praying for You."

Samuel had the heartbeat of an intercessor when he told the people of Israel, "Far be it from me that I should sin against the LORD in ceasing to pray for you" (1 Sam. 12:23). Nothing can compare to the encouragement we feel when we learn that someone has been praying for us. We can pass along the same power of intercessory prayer by praying for others. There are three groups of people for whom we can pray as intercessors:

1. For Other Believers

In his letter to the Ephesians, Paul offers us a glimpse into his own intercessory prayer life. By describing in detail how he prayed for other Christians, Paul provides us a model of intercession for fellow believers. As you pray for your brothers and sisters in Christ, here are some things the book of Ephesians teaches us to include:

- Give thanks for their salvation (1:16).
- Ask that God would give them wisdom and knowledge of Himself (1:17).
- Pray that they would understand the hope and the riches of God's salvation (1:18).
- Pray that they would recognize God's mighty power in their lives (1:19).
- Pray that God would grant them inner strength (3:16).
- Ask that Christ would abide in their hearts through faith (3:17).
- Pray that they would be able to stand firm and comprehend the full measure of Christ's love (3:18–19).
- Pray that they would be filled with all the fullness of God (3:19).
- Pray that they would be used to God's glory (3:20).

2. For People in Leadership

Paul wrote, "I exhort first of all that supplications, prayers, intercessions, and giving of thanks be made for all men, for kings and all who are in authority, that we may lead a quiet and peaceable life in all godliness and reverence" (1 Tim. 2:1–2).

God has established the importance of praying for other people, and specifically has emphasized the need to pray for those in leadership. For the sake of the advancement of the gospel and the peace of the church, God's people should pray for the president/prime minister, legislators, other political and military leaders, and those in local government, as well as those who are accountable for the church.

As we pray for leaders in government, education, the military, business, and the community, we can ask . . .

- that unsaved leaders will come to know Christ.
- that leaders would honor God in their actions.
- that leaders would seek God's wisdom in the decisions they make.

- that the Lord would bring peace and prosperity to the nation so that the gospel might be shared with freedom.

Beyond praying for leaders in the culture and society, we should uphold the pastors and other spiritual leaders in our churches. For spiritual leaders, we can pray that these leaders will . . .

- maintain close fellowship with Jesus.
- grow in knowledge of God and His Word.
- have a clear vision for the ministry.
- display the fruit of the Spirit.
- honor God in their families.
- depend on Christ's wisdom.

3. For Unsaved People

A complete approach to evangelism involves communication in two directions. We must talk to people about Jesus. We also must talk to God about people. Certainly we want to be faithful and passionate in sharing the good news of Christ with the lost people around us. If our work in soul winning is not accompanied with prayer, however, our efforts will lack the fullness of the Holy Spirit's power.

Prayer for lost people should include the following petitions:

- *Pray that they will hear the message of Jesus.* When Paul arrived at the city of Philippi, he met Lydia, who worshipped God but who did not have a relationship with Jesus. As Paul shared the message of Christ with her, "the Lord opened her heart to heed the things spoken by Paul" (Acts 16:14). As we pray for lost people, we can ask for God to prepare them to receive the gospel. We can pray that the social, mental, and spiritual barriers would come down.
- *Pray that their eyes will be able to see their own sin.* Satan has blinded the lost so that they cannot see the light of Christ or their need to be saved (2 Cor. 4:4). We can pray for God's Holy

Spirit to convict them of their sin, of God's righteousness, and of God's coming judgment (John 16:8).

- *Pray that their hearts will turn to Jesus.* Repentance is spiritually turning away from sin and turning toward Jesus. God grants lost people repentance so they can escape the snare of Satan and know the truth of Christ (2 Tim. 2:25–26). As we pray for unsaved friends, we can ask that God would give them grace to turn toward Jesus so they can receive eternal life in His name.

Evangelistic prayer involves praying for nonbelievers and for Christian witnesses. We can pray that witnesses have strength to share their faith boldly and with confidence (Acts 4:29–31), even in difficult and dangerous circumstances. We can pray for open opportunities to share (Col. 4:2–6), for Christian lives that are consistent with the gospel (Acts 10:38), and for protection of the message and messenger from the Evil One (John 17:15).

Getting Involved

Christians who are serious about intercession will find ways to establish a meaningful prayer ministry. Here are some practical ways to become involved in intercessory prayer:

- *Establish a permanent prayer list of people you commit to pray for.* This list may include family, friends, church leaders, missionaries, leaders in your community and city, and national leaders. Make it a practice to pray through this list on a regular basis. Make requests for specific needs in the life of each person for whom you are praying.
- *Keep a weekly or monthly list of current needs for prayer.* This list should contain the names of people who have pressing concerns. It should include the names of those who are sick, those troubled at work or in their families, and those who need spiritual life or growth in grace. You may want to list these items with space for recording answers to petitions.

- *Get involved with others in intercessory prayer.* Your church may have an intercessory prayer ministry to join. If not, consider starting a ministry of intercession in your congregation. God honors churches that take prayer seriously, and God will bless believers who make time for others.

SHOULD I PRAY FOR HEALING?

In the corridors of a hospital, a pastor was stopped by a man who wanted to ask the most common of questions relating to sickness. "Pastor," he said, "do you believe in divine healing?"

"Is there any other kind?" his pastor responded wisely. "Does anyone heal but God? The doctor can prescribe, and the surgeon can cut, and the emergency room physician can sew up the wound, but only God can heal."

Some Christians feel uncomfortable praying for God to heal their own bodies or others in physical distress. Some believers grow discouraged, disappointed, or angry after praying for healing that doesn't come.

What does the Bible have to say about praying for healing? Here we will give only a cursory summary of biblical teaching on prayer and physical healing, but five simple principles might help us get a better handle on this subject.

1. God Is Able to Heal.

God affirms that He can heal the sick. He promised to protect His people from the diseases He had brought upon the Egyptians, so long as the Israelites obeyed Him. He told them, "I am the LORD who heals you" (Exod. 15:26). Moses prayed for his sister, Miriam, and she was healed of leprosy (Num. 12:9–13). Naaman, commander in the Syrian army, also was healed of leprosy through his faith in God (2 Kings 5:1–19). When King Hezekiah was near death, he prayed for God to extend his life, and he received God's healing (Isa. 38:1–8).

The Lord Jesus sometimes restored people merely by speaking a word. At other times, Jesus touched people or even used clay made with His own saliva to bring about healing. Matthew records a typical day in the life of Jesus, writing, "When evening had come, they brought to Him many who were demon-possessed. And He cast out the spirits with a word, and healed all who were sick" (Matt. 8:16). Jesus accomplished healing as part of His messianic mission, "that it might be fulfilled which was spoken by Isaiah the prophet, saying: 'He Himself took our infirmities and bore our sicknesses'" (Matt. 8:17). Jesus gave His disciples authority to heal, and their healing ministry validated the gospel message they proclaimed (Matt. 10:1–8).

Healing flows from God's character. Because God is all-powerful, He has the ability to heal. Because He is all-knowing, He has the insight to heal. Because He is all-loving, He has the compassion to heal. Because He is gracious and merciful, He has the desire to heal.

2. God Invites Believers to Pray for Healing.

God has instructed Christians to ask Him to grant healing. "Is anyone among you sick? Let him call for the elders of the church, and let them pray over him, anointing him with oil in the name of the Lord. And the prayer of faith will save the sick, and the Lord will raise him up. And if he has committed sins, he will be forgiven" (James 5:14–15).

Several things are notable about these verses:

- *The request for prayer is initiated by the sick person, who is instructed to ask for prayer.*
- *The prayer for healing takes place within the fellowship of the church.* The spiritual leaders pray and anoint with oil as representatives of the local body of Christ.
- *The prayer for healing is accompanied by anointing.* Oil symbolized God's merciful anointing in prayer and healing. It also

may have had medicinal applications. We should avoid two extremes: One is to pray with faith and refuse medical attention. The other is to seek medical help, but never pray.

- *The prayer is offered in faith.* Those who pray for healing must come to God with the conviction that God is able to heal and with the willingness to risk making a bold request.
- *The prayer includes spiritual as well as physical restoration.* James includes the spiritual component that can accompany illness. If a sick person has committed sins, prayer will bring about forgiveness.

God's Word encourages us to pray for healing. He can do amazing things. We must be careful, however, not to mistake God's invitation as a guarantee that He will always answer by taking away the problem. Praying in faith involves leaving our requests in His hands. God is loving, generous, all-wise, and sovereign.

3. Sickness, Pain, and Death Are Realities.

Suffering is an inescapable fact of human life. Sometimes physical ailments come as a result of our own choices. We eat the wrong things and we get sick. We live an unhealthy lifestyle and develop problems as a result. Other physical troubles occur because we live in an imperfect world where we can come to harm. A teenager dislocates his shoulder on the football field. A person develops cancer after exposure to a carcinogen.

Illness may come as a result of God's discipline. "For whom the Lord loves He chastens, and scourges every son whom He receives" (Heb. 12:6). God allows some physical problems only so that He may be glorified. Jesus's disciples once asked Him why a certain man was born blind. Jesus answered, "Neither this man nor his parents sinned, but that the works of God should be revealed in him" (John 9:2–3). Though God calls us to ask for healing when we are sick, He has not made believers immune from sickness, pain, and death.

4. God Does Not Always Heal When We Ask.

Christians become sick, get injured, and die. Christian parents praying for a sick child experience heartache if prayer does not result in deliverance. Prayer does not always deliver us from suffering.

The apostle Paul referred to some type of physical problem, which he called his "thorn in the flesh." Three times he asked God to deliver him from the problem. Instead of healing Paul, God had another purpose—to use the thorn in the flesh for His glory: "He said to me, 'My grace is sufficient for you, for My strength is made perfect in weakness'" (2 Cor. 12:9a). Based on what the Lord showed him, Paul wrote: "Therefore most gladly I will rather boast in my infirmities, that the power of Christ may rest upon me" (v. 9b).

Though we are not always delivered from pain and death on earth, God has promised a coming day for believers when He will wipe away every tear from our eyes, when "there shall be no more death, nor sorrow, nor crying" (Rev. 21:4). When God does not answer our requests for healing as we had expected, we can rest confidently in His promise of ultimate healing in heaven.

5. Prayers for Healing Should Be Made in Submission.

Learning to say, "Nevertheless not My will, but Yours, be done" (Luke 22:42) is especially important when we are praying for healing. We can pray confidently and boldly for healing. We can say, "Lord, I am asking for a full recovery with no complications. I am asking for total healing in this situation. Even so, Your will be done, Lord."

Praying this way is not "hedging our bets" in case healing doesn't come. It's simply a recognition that God is in control and knows the bigger picture. God works through prayers and answers prayers, and He desires us to pray for healing. Yet we recognize that everything that happens is subject to His will.

HOW SHOULD I TEACH MY CHILD TO PRAY?

"God is great. God is good.
Let us thank Him for our food. . . ." [8]
"Now I lay me down to sleep;
I pray the Lord my soul to keep. . . ." [9]

Perhaps you learned those simple prayers as a child. You may have taught your children to use similar children's prayers at mealtime and bedtime. While there's nothing wrong with those prayers in themselves, they come short of teaching our children how to call on God in prayer. Many parents ask, "How can I teach my child to pray?"

An older friend once gave us some good advice on parenting. "Always remember," he said, "your goal is not to raise up a child but to raise up an adult." This person was exactly right. Our aim for our children is that they become adults who follow Christ. If our children are to be people who know the importance of prayer and who make prayer a daily practice, parents and grandparents must teach them to pray. Andrew Murray commented that "If we do not learn how to pray when we are younger, we will stumble at it all of our lives." [10]

Here are three ways to teach children to pray.

First, we can let our children see and hear us praying. Children pay attention to our example, and they tend to imitate what they see. When they see us begin each day with prayer, they are learning about the priority of prayer. When they hear us pray for wisdom and guidance in times of crisis, they are being trained to rely on prayer for God's direction.

Fathers should be especially aware of their children's need to see them praying. Too often, dads neglect to provide a visible model of devotion to prayer, which may lead sons in particular to think that praying is something that women do, but not men. By setting an example of genuinely calling out to God in prayer, we teach our sons and daughters that prayer has real meaning and purpose, and that it can have that same importance in their lives.

Second, we can pray with our children. Parents should set aside a daily time for Bible reading and prayer, starting a habit of prayer that our children can continue throughout their lives. This family devotional time does not need to be long, especially when children are very young. Nor does this time need to include a lot of detailed instruction. We simply need to set aside a brief but meaningful time every day to pray and read God's Word together with our families. Younger children may find it useful to have tangible things they can touch and hold as they pray. For instance, photographs of family members, missionaries, teachers, and church leaders may help boys and girls focus on the people for whom they are praying.

In addition to a family devotional time, parents should look for other occasions to pray with children about their problems, about upcoming tests at school, about decisions they have to make, and about other parts of their lives. When children know that their parents will pray with them, they are more likely to bring up prayer requests for the family to pray about. As we pray with our children, it gives us opportunities to teach them about how God works through prayer. They will discover that God sometimes answers prayers in ways we don't expect. They will also learn how to pray patiently and to wait on God's timing.

Third, we can teach our children patterns for prayer. A memorized prayer can hinder a child from learning to pray, since children may tend to substitute reciting for praying. Teaching our children simple patterns for prayer, however, can help remind them of what to include as they pray.

For younger children, a helpful pattern may be to pray using the letters J-O-Y. *J* reminds the child to begin by praising *Jesus*. *O* stands for *others* and their needs. *Y* stands for *yourself*, and teaches children to confess their sins and make requests for personal needs. During prayer time, parents can prompt children to pray for each of these areas.

The "fingers of prayer" reminder can help older children pray:

- The *thumb* is the nearest to you. Begin your prayers by praying for those who are closest to you. They are the easiest to remember.

- The next finger is the *pointing finger.* Pray for those who teach, instruct, and heal. This includes teachers, doctors, and ministers.
- The next finger is the *tallest finger.* Pray for leaders to receive God's guidance and wisdom.
- The *ring finger* is the weakest finger. It reminds us to pray for those who are weak, in trouble, or in pain.
- The *little finger* reminds us to pray last for ourselves. By the time we have prayed for the needs of others, our own needs will be put into proper perspective, and we will be able to pray for ourselves more effectively.

By praying with our children, by modeling a faithful life of prayer, and by teaching children how to pray, parents magnify God in our families. The Lord will honor parents' efforts to bring up our children "in the training and admonition of the Lord" (Eph. 6:4).

HOW CAN I PRAY TO BECOME A CHRISTIAN?

God's gift of salvation and eternal life comes in answer to prayer. God says, "Whoever calls on the name of the LORD shall be saved" (Rom. 10:13). What does it mean to "call on the name of the LORD"? Calling on Jesus for salvation involves understanding and believing several things.

1. *Sin separates us from God.* "All have sinned and fall short of the glory of God" (Rom. 3:23). Sin is anything about us that displeases God. We may sin in the things we say, in the things we do, or even in the things we think. Every person has sinned, and deserves eternal separation from God in hell because of sin. "The wages of sin is death, but the gift of God is eternal life in Christ Jesus our Lord" (Rom. 6:23).
2. *Jesus paid the price for our sin.* "God so loved the world that He gave His only begotten Son, that whoever believes in Him should not perish but have everlasting life" (John 3:16). Jesus—

God's eternal Son—lived a perfect life. He never sinned. When Jesus was crucified on the cross, He died in our place for our sins. God sent Jesus to die for us because He loves us. "God demonstrates His own love toward us, in that while we were still sinners, Christ died for us" (Rom. 5:8).

3. *Salvation is found in Jesus alone.* "By grace you have been saved through faith, and that not of yourselves; it is the gift of God, not of works, lest anyone should boast" (Eph. 2:8–9). Our goodness, morality, or religious activity will not make us right with God. By His grace, God saves us when we place our trust in Jesus. Only by faith in Jesus Christ can a person be saved. "Nor is there salvation in any other, for there is no other name under heaven given among men by which we must be saved" (Acts 4:12).

4. *We must trust Jesus personally.* In order to receive the gift of salvation, we must call on Christ. It's not enough just to know the truth about who Jesus is and what He did on the cross. It's not even sufficient to say, "Yes, I accept that all of these things about my sin and Jesus's death and resurrection are true." Salvation requires turning from sin and asking for the Lord to save us. "If you confess with your mouth the Lord Jesus and believe in your heart that God has raised Him from the dead, you will be saved" (Rom. 10:9).

The truth of the gospel is simple, but trusting in Jesus for salvation will change your eternity. God's greatest desire for you is to have eternal life with Him through His Son. If you would like to have a relationship with Jesus Christ, you can call on the Lord right now by simply praying a prayer like this:

Dear Lord Jesus, I know I am a sinner. I believe You died for my sins. Right now, I turn from my sins and ask for Your salvation. I trust You as my Lord and Savior. Thank You for saving me. Amen.

If you have prayed that prayer and meant it in your heart, Jesus Christ has saved you. Remember God's promise: "Whoever calls on the name of the Lord shall be saved." Your decision to call on Jesus for salvation means that God has forgiven you of your sins and that you will spend eternity with Him.

Once you place your faith in Christ, you become a child of God, and you have the privilege of talking to Him in prayer, at any time, about anything. He will fill your life with purpose as you seek Him in prayer.

NOTES

Introduction

1. "*U.S. News* and Beliefnet Prayer Survey Results," reporting on a survey conducted by *U.S. News and World Report* and beliefnet.com. beliefnet.com/story/157/story_15791 (accessed December 20, 2004).
2. Ibid.

Day 1: A Life Filled with Prayer

1. E. M. Bounds, "The Reality of Prayer," in *The Complete Works of E. M. Bounds on Prayer* (Grand Rapids: Baker, 1990), 253.

Day 2: While He Prayed

1. Wayne Grudem, *Systematic Theology: An Introduction to Biblical Doctrine* (Grand Rapids: Zondervan, 1994), 377.
2. Story related to the author by Suzanne Rape, a niece of the couple.
3. Wayne Grudem, *Systematic Theology: An Introduction to Biblical Doctrine* (Grand Rapids: Zondervan, 1994), 377.
4. David Popenoe, "Life Without Father: Disappearing Dads Are Destroying Our Future," *Utne* Magazine online (1999 archives),

reprinted from *Wilson Quarterly*, September-October 1996 at Utne.com/pub/1999_77/features/700-1 (accessed December 13, 2005).

5. Charles Schultz, "Peanuts," n.d., copyright United Features Syndicate.

Day 3: He Often Withdrew and Prayed

1. Quoted in Edythe Draper, *Draper's Book of Quotations for the Christian World* (Wheaton: Tyndale House, 1992), entry 8816.

2. Quoted in "Colorful Sayings from Colorful Moody," Christianity Today Online, ctlibrary.com/3689 (accessed December 19, 2005).

3. Jean Fleming, "How Busy Is Too Busy?" *Decision*, March 1988, 16–17.

4. James Stalker, *The Life of Christ* (New York: Revell, 1949), 104.

5. Martin Luther, *A Simple Way to Pray* (1535), quoted in "How I Pray: Counsel on Approaching the Almighty," in "Martin Luther—The Later Years and Legacy," *Christian History & Biography* (July 1993).

Day 4: Ask . . . Seek . . . Knock

1. Phillips Brooks, quoted in "WatchCry Quotes: Provoking Thoughts on Prayer, Revival, and Missions," sermonindex.net/modules/newbb/viewtopic.php?topic_id=6690&forum=40&2 (accessed November 1, 2005).

2. Quoted in Mark Water, ed., *The Encyclopedia of Prayer and Praise* (Peabody, MA: Hendrickson, 2004), 1146.

3. John Maxwell, *Partners in Prayer* (Nashville: Nelson, 1996), 23.

Day 5: In Jesus's Name

1. R. A. Torrey, *How to Pray* (1900), reprinted in R. A. Torrey, *Power-Filled Living: How to Receive God's Best for Your Life* (New Kensington, PA: Whitaker House, 1998), 296.

2. Ibid.

3. James Montgomery Boice, *The Gospel of John: An Expositional Commentary*, vol. 4, *Peace in the Storm* (Grand Rapids: Baker, 1999), 1103.

4. Ralph L. Keiper and James M. Boice, *Is Prayer a Problem?* (Philadelphia: Bible Study Hour, 1974), 23.

Day 6: Not As I Will, but As You Will

1. Quoted in Mark Water, ed., *The Encyclopedia of Prayer and Praise* (Peabody, MA: Hendrickson, 2004), 1152.
2. Charles Stanley, *The Wonderful, Spirit-Filled Life* (Nashville: Nelson, 1992), 49.
3. Richard J. Foster, "Crucifying Our Will: Praying Through the Struggle to Let Go," *Knowing and Doing*, fall 2005: 1–4. This publication of the C. S. Lewis Institute is available online at cslewisinstitute.org/pages/resources/publications/knowingDoing/2005/CrucifyingOurWill (accessed December 19, 2005).
4. Quoted in Edythe Draper, *Draper's Book of Quotations for the Christian World* (Wheaton: Tyndale House, 1992), entry 10972.

Day 9: Praying Through Pain

1. C. S. Lewis, *The Problem of Pain* (1940; rep. ed., San Francisco: HarperSanFrancisco, 2001), 91.
2. Adrian Rogers, *God's Hidden Treasures* (Wheaton: Tyndale, 1999), 11.
3. Jim George, *The Remarkable Prayers of the Bible* (Eugene, OR: Harvest House, 2005), 46.
4. Quoted in Iain Murray, "Robert Murray M'Cheyne" at graceonlinelibrary.org/articles/full.asp?id=38%7c%7c442 (accessed December 19, 2005).
5. Kenneth W. Osbeck, *Amazing Grace: 366 Inspiring Hymn Stories for Daily Devotions* (Grand Rapids: Kregel, 1990), March 18.

Day 10: Falling into God's Arms

1. Quoted in *Leadership* 16, no. 3 (Summer 1995).

Day 11: Trusting God's Timing

1. Thomas Watson, *Gleanings from Thomas Watson* (Morgan, PA: Soli Deo Gloria, 1995), 99.

Day 12: Praising Our God

1. Matthew Henry, *Commentary on the Whole Bible, Complete and Unabridged in One Volume* (rep. ed., Peabody, MA: Hendrickson, 1991), commentary for 1 Sam. 2:1.

Day 13: Recognizing God's Sovereignty

1. Quoted in A. W. Pink, *The Attributes of God* (repr. ed., Grand Rapids: Baker, 1999), 32–33.
2. Adapted from Susan C. Kimber, "Heart to Heart," in *Today's Christian Woman.*
3. Lois Spoon, "Divine Calculation: My Prayer Was Answered by Someone's Pocket Change," *Today's Christian* (September–October 1999), christianitytoday.com/tc/9r5/9r5059 (accessed December 19, 2005).
4. For the story of the Cullinan Diamonds, see the Famous Diamonds Web site, famousdiamonds.tripod.com/cullinandiamonds (accessed November 2, 2005).

Day 15: Praying Through a Failure

1. Randy Kennedy, *"Jeopardy!* Whiz Ken Jennings Loses," *New York Times*, 1 December 2004.

Day 16: When All Systems Fail

1. Quoted in Bill Turpie, *Ten Great Preachers* (Grand Rapids: Odyssey Productions, 2000), 97.
2. Ibid.

3. Alan Redpath, *The Making of a Man of God* (Grand Rapids: Revell, 1990), 241.
4. Charles Swindoll, *David: A Story of Passion and Destiny*, Great Lives from God's Word (Nashville: W Publishing Group, 1997), 1:205–6.
5. Condoleezza Rice, "Opening Statement to the 9/11 Commission, April 8, 2004," edition.cnn.com/2004/ALLPOLITICS/04/08/rice.transcript (accessed October 10, 2005).

Day 17: Coming Clean with God

1. Charles Haddon Spurgeon, *The Treasury of David* (Grand Rapids: Kregel, 1976), 238.
2. "Unwashed for 10 Years, Smelly Kenyan Gets Scrubdown," abc.net.au/news/newsitems/s1060469.htm (accessed September 15, 2005).

Day 18: Moving Forward from Failure

1. Quoted from J. Hudson Taylor's personal testimony in Lee Robertson, *The Faith That Moves Mountains* (Murfreesboro, TN: Sword of the Lord, 2000), 41.
2. See Erwin W. Lutzer, *Failure, the Backdoor to Success* (Chicago: Moody, 1975), 82–84.

Day 19: Guilt-Free Living

1. Corrie ten Boom, *Not Good if Detached* (Fort Washington, PA: Christian Literature Crusade, 1957), 19.
2. Adapted from Virgil Hurley, *Speaker's Sourcebook of New Illustrations* (Dallas: Word, 1995), 94.
3. Thomas Szasz, *The Untamed Tongue: A Dissenting Dictionary* (Chicago: Open Court, 1990), 138.
4. Adapted from Robert J. Morgan, *Nelson's Complete Book of Stories, Illustrations, and Quotes* (Nashville: Nelson, 2000), 367–68.

5. Tom Blair in *San Diego Union*, quoted in *Reader's Digest*. Blair is a collector of urban legends, and this story likely has no factual basis.

6. Rosalind Goforth, *Climbing* (Wheaton: Sword Book Club, 1940), 90.

Day 20: How to Make Failure Fail

1. Quoted at heprayed.com/quotes (accessed December 20, 2005).

Day 23: Our Father's Holy Name

1. Max Lucado, *The Great House of God* (Dallas: Word, 1997), 21.

2. David Jeremiah, *Prayer: The Great Adventure* (Sisters, OR: Multnomah, 1997), 90.

3. Joachim Jeremias, *The Prayers of Jesus* (New York: SCM, 1967), 57.

4. William Barclay, *The Gospel of Matthew* (Philadelphia: Westminster, 1975), 1:205.

5. Donald W. McCullough, *The Trivialization of God* (Colorado Springs: NavPress, 1995), 112.

6. Charles H. Spurgeon, *Morning and Evening: Daily Readings* (Oak Harbor, WA: Logos Research Systems, 1995), October 29 AM.

Day 24: Our Father's Coming Kingdom

1. Clarence Edward Macartney, *Macartney's Illustrations* (New York: Abingdon, 1946), 409.

2. R. G. Lee, "Payday—Someday," in *Payday—Someday and Other Sermons by Robert Greene Lee*, ed. Timothy and Denise George (Nashville: Broadman and Holman, 1995), 23.

3. Adapted from John MacArthur, "Thy Kingdom Come," in *Alone with God* (Wheaton: Victor, 1995).

4. Elisabeth Elliot, *The Shadow of the Almighty: The Life and Testament of Jim Elliot* (New York: Harper and Row, 1958), 108.

5. Ibid., 196.

6. David Jeremiah, *Prayer: The Great Adventure* (Sisters, OR: Multnomah, 1997), 135.

7. Ricky Skaggs, "Deep Roots," *Guideposts*, August 2003, 60–64.

8. Ricky Skaggs, "Following by Faith, Not Feelings," skaggsfamilyre-cords.com/mission.cfm?CFID=6188920&CFTOKEN=77083900 (accessed October 13, 2005).

Day 25: Our Father's Constant Care

1. D. L. Moody, quoted in *Our Daily Bread* (December 30, 1985).

2. Bill Hybels, *Too Busy Not to Pray* (Downers Grove, IL: InterVarsity, 1998), 31.

3. Used by the Huron Hunger Fund, Diocese of Huron, Ontario, Anglican Church of Canada, n.d.

4. Lewis B. Smedes, *Forgive and Forget* (New York: Simon and Schuster, 1984), 14.

Day 26: Our Father's Delivering Power

1. John A. Shedd, *Salt from My Attic* (Portland, ME: Mosher Press, 1928).

2. Bill Bryson, "Life's Little Gambles," *Saturday Evening Post*, September 1988.

3. James Emory White, *The Prayer God Longs For* (Downers Grove, IL: InterVarsity, 2005), 90.

4. C. S. Lewis, *The Screwtape Letters* (New York: Macmillan, 1961), 9.

Day 27: Our Father's Surpassing Glory

1. Charles Wesley, "O, for a Thousand Tongues to Sing" (1739).

2. J. I. Packer, *Knowing God* (Downers Grove, IL: InterVarsity, 1973), 18.

3. John N. Oswalt, "Chabod," in *Theological Wordbook of the Old Testament,* ed. R. L. Harris, G. L. Archer Jr., and B. K. Waltke (Chicago: Moody, 1980).

4. Washington Irving, *The Legend of Sleepy Hollow and Other Stories in the Sketch Book* (New York: Signet, 1990), 332.

5. Wayne Grudem, *Systematic Theology* (Grand Rapids: Zondervan, 1994), 221.

6. A. W. Tozer, *The Knowledge of the Holy* (San Francisco: HarperCollins, 1961), 1.

7. Quoted in Terry Mattingly, "When Did Bach Find Time to Pray?" *Adoremus Bulletin*, online edition, 6.8 (November 2000). Adoremus Society for the Reverence of the Sacred Liturgy, online edition (accessed at adoremus.org/11-00-mattingly).

Appendix: Crucial Questions About Prayer

1. George MacDonald, quoted in Kent and Barbara Hughes, *Liberating Ministry from the Success Syndrome* (Wheaton: Tyndale, 1988), 72.

2. Adapted from Oliver W. Price, *The Power of Praying Together: Experiencing Christ Actively in Charge* (Grand Rapids: Kregel, 1999), 12.

3. Wesley L. Duewel, *Mighty Prevailing Prayer* (Grand Rapids: Zondervan, 1990), 32.

4. D. Martyn Lloyd-Jones, *Preaching and Preachers* (Grand Rapids: Zondervan, 1972), 170.

5. Oswald Chambers, *Christian Disciplines: Containing the Disciplines of Divine Guidance, Suffering, Peril, Prayer, Loneliness, Patience* (London: Marshall, Morgan & Scott, 1936).

6. P. T. Forsyth, *The Soul of Prayer* (Grand Rapids: Eerdmans, 1916), 14.

7. C. H. Spurgeon, *Morning and Evening: Daily Readings*, electronic version (Oak Harbor, WA: Logos Research Systems, 1995), March 29 PM.

8. Traditional child's prayer, origin not known.

9. Benjamin West, ed., *The New England Primer* (1683).

10. Andrew Murray, quoted in *Christianity Today*, 5 February 1990, 38.

ABOUT THE AUTHORS

Stephen Nelson Rummage (Ph. D., New Orleans Baptist Theological Seminary; M.Div., Southeastern Baptist Theological Seminary) is preaching pastor at Hickory Grove Baptist Church in Charlotte, North Carolina. He also serves as an adjunctive professor of preaching at Southeastern Seminary in Wake Forest, North Carolina. Dr. Rummage is the author of *Planning Your Preaching* (Kregel, 2002).

Michele Henderson Rummage (M.A., Christian Education, New Orleans Baptist Theological Seminary) has conducted seminars on Christian marriage and the family in local churches. She has mentored and taught courses for wives of seminary students. The Rummages have one son, Joshua.